# HOW TO
# DOUBLE
## YOUR
# SALES
## BY
# ASKING A
# FEW MORE
# QUESTIONS

*Making More Sales by
Helping People Get
What They Really Want*

## SIDNEY C. WALKER

Author of

*Trusting Yourself & The Prospecting Mentality*

Formatting Supervision by Tom Raddemann
Cover Design by Robert L. Schram


10 9 8 7 6 5 4 3 2 1

Printed in the United States of America.


ISBN 0-9621177-1-4

# *Dedication*

To Phil Kline — For skillfully teaching me to ask the feeling-oriented questions.

# *Author's Note*

Welcome to a great adventure.

This book has everything it needs to get the job done. I say that with confidence because I've been teaching this information and getting great results for over 14 years.

This book is concise and to the point yet a lot is covered. Give yourself the gift of some quality time to read this book and take your time. I promise you that your time will be well invested.

For simplicity's sake, I have used the plural pronouns of "they" and "them" as much as possible throughout the book instead of "he" and "she," "him" and "her," etc. Also, I have used the term "prospective client," realizing that in many cases the word "client" could be easily interchanged.

This material can profoundly impact your life. It is written from a context much bigger than just asking feeling-oriented questions, although that is the subject matter. From a bigger perspective, this book is about continuing to learn to shift from a state of *fear and doubt* to a state of *trust and faith* toward life's creative process. Being able to make this shift is critical to our evolution. I wish every reader the greatest success in this endeavor.

*SID WALKER*

Longmont, Colorado

# *Contents*

Author's Note

# *Chapter 1*

## WHAT
## THIS
## INFORMATION
## CAN
## DO
## FOR
## YOU

## AN OVERVIEW

This book will make clear the importance of getting your prospective clients to a feeling level in the sales interview. It will tell you why we tend to shy away from asking the feeling-oriented questions and what you can do about it. It will detail numerous ways to make it easier and more comfortable for both you and your prospective clients to get to a feeling level. A variety of scenarios are presented to give you a feel for what it is like to get to a feeling level. Finally, you will be given information that will help you deal with the uncertainties inherent in asking feeling-oriented questions. In total, this book is a manual on how to help your prospective clients get clear about what *they* really want so you can help them get it. The proven results of this approach are more sales for you and more satisfied clients.

## YOU CAN FEEL THE DIFFERENCE

It has been said in many ways that people buy based on emotion (feelings) and not just on logic. Or that what people *want* is a greater motivator than what they *need*. Yet if we could listen in on most sales interviews and presentations, getting to an emotional (feeling) level with the prospective client more often happens by accident than by design.

My contention is that your prospective clients cannot make a decision to buy your product or service unless it feels right to them. Fortunately, many prospective clients figure this out on their own and make a buying decision. Unfortunately, many prospective clients do not know how to determine what would feel right to them, and very often the salesperson doesn't know how to help prospective clients determine what feels right. The net result is that no sale is made. Your prospective clients will politely say they want to think about it.

Guess why they want to think about it? Usually because they aren't really clear about what they want and why they would want it in relation to your product or service. I believe, if your prospective clients are really clear about what they want and why they want it, most can and will make a decision one way or another.

## A Good Reason Isn't Enough

I have worked with over 1,000 individual clients in the past 14 years; most have been salespeople selling financial services. You would be amazed at the number of veteran salespeople who complain to me that they have a lot of business pending but they can't seem to get people to stop putting them off and make a decision. The less experienced salespeople will often tell me they can get in the door and establish relationships with people, but they are not able to close as many sales as they would like.

In both situations I ask the salespeople to tell me about their prospective clients. I ask them, "Tell me what your prospective client wants and why he wants it." I will usually get a barrage of facts about their situation. Then I say: "Okay, the guy wants his children to be guaranteed that they can go to college in case he dies prematurely. Good. Now why does he want that?" Most salespeople I talk to get a blank look on their face and tell me they don't know. They don't know why the prospective client wants to guarantee that his children can go to college, and they don't know why because they never asked. And they never asked because most salespeople figure that wanting to make sure your children can go to college is enough of a reason to buy, in this case, life insurance. It's true, it's a great reason, but it isn't a feeling, and it is feelings that move people to action. How strongly your prospective clients feel about what they want will determine how fast they take action.

The feeling comes out when you ask your prospective clients why they want to be sure their children can go to college. Even though this may sound like a question with an obvious answer, if you take the time to ask the question, you will be surprised at the answers you will get.

## What Gene Really Wanted

I had a client in this exact situation who asked his prospective client, Gene, why he wanted to be sure his children could go to college. Gene said: "I *couldn't* go to college and it took me a lot longer to establish myself and get a good paying job. I know I lost a lot of money in the early years of my career because I didn't have a college education. Life is hard enough without having dis-advantages. I want my kids to have every advantage pos-sible so they can have the security of good jobs."

Can you hear some emotion in Gene's response? You can sense that Gene struggled because he didn't have a college education and he doesn't want his kids to have to struggle like he did. He wants to make sure that they have the advantage of a college education and the increased pay that it warrants.

So let's say Salesperson A goes back to see Gene to close him on a program to guarantee that his kids can go to college if he dies prematurely. If the only information Salesperson A got from Gene was that he wanted to make sure his kids could go to college, all he can present in the closing interview is how the program works, which is all logic, and hope he wants to buy it.

Now let's say Salesperson B remembered to ask Gene why he wants to guarantee his children can go to college. Salesperson B could start the closing interview like this:

B:	"Gene, the last time we talked you told me you wanted to guarantee that your children would have the money to go to college no matter what happened to you. Is that right?"

Gene:	"Yes."

B:	"You also said that you struggled financially because you couldn't go to college and you don't want your children to have to struggle like you did. You said life is hard enough without having disadvantages, and you want to give them every advantage you can so they can get good jobs. Is that right?"

Gene:	"That is exactly right!"

B:	"Let me show you a plan that will give you everything we've talked about...."

Who do you think has a better chance of selling Gene? Salesperson A with logic only, or Salesperson B who has the logic and the feeling-level information? Obviously Salesperson B, right? Because Salesperson B knows what Gene wants and why he wants it and can remind Gene of what he said he wanted in his closing presentation.

**The Bottom Line**

In my research and observations of closing ratios over the years with my clients, the numbers have been very consistent. If you try to close with logic only, you will close around 25-30% of your closing presentations. If you close with logic *and* emotion, namely, knowing what your prospective clients want and why they want it, you will double your closing ratio to 60%. I've seen many closing ratios go much higher using this approach.

So if you could more than double your closing ratio by asking a few more questions, would you be willing to ask a few more questions? You're probably saying, "Okay, that sounds good, but what are the questions?" That's the focus of this material: getting you skilled and comfortable at asking the feeling-level questions.

## WHAT YOU CAN GAIN FROM THIS MATERIAL

If you doubled your income, you'd have the benefit of having a lot of extra money in your bank account, and I trust you'd be able to find something to spend it on.

Many times I have had salespeople say to me, "I want to be a stronger closer, but I want a more elegant way to close." Or, "I want to be able to ask the hard questions and I want to be able to motivate people to act, but I don't want to have to 'beat them up' in the process." Or, "When I push people, I feel terrible and they feel terrible." Knowing what your prospective clients want and why they want it is the most powerful and elegant approach there is. It is a counseling-style approach where everybody wins.

- Can you imagine what it would be like to have an approach to your sales process that made you want to jump out of bed in the morning?

- Can you imagine helping people make wise decisions and as a result having them buy a ton of your product or service?

- Can you imagine feeling good about yourself because you are really helping people and having them actually thank you for your help?

- Can you imagine what it would feel like to be truly appreciated by hundreds of people?

- Can you imagine what it would be like to be doing business in a way that empowers you and makes you feel good at the deepest level?

More money, a more elegant way to get people to take action, having your clients feel good about you, and you feeling great about yourself — those are the payoffs for asking a few more questions.

## HOW TO GET THE MOST OUT OF THIS INFORMATION

Remember that learning new skills can be challenging, but the rewards will far outweigh the effort.

Keep an open mind as you go through this text. Give your internal critic a rest for at least one time through. Keep in mind that *you are not going to do everything exactly the way I do it* and you don't need to. The key is to **understand the essence of what is being presented and then experiment to find your own style or version of this approach.**

I recommend that you reread this material as many times as it takes to totally absorb the information. Some parts are going to have more meaning to you than others. Focus on those parts that have more meaning. You will begin to see subtle but important adjustments to make in your fact-finding and feeling-finding process with your prospective clients.

This material is designed to create a mentality that will close more sales with a feeling of integrity and personal well-being. You will know when you've got it because you will be able to feel it. If you are feeling good about yourself and the approach you are taking with your prospective clients, good things are going to happen. Learn the information presented, risk asking a few more questions, and I promise you the increase in your sales will be well worth the time invested.

# *Chapter 2*

# WHY
# PEOPLE
# BUY

## HOW WE MAKE DECISIONS

In order to better understand what actually needs to happen for your prospective client to make a buying decision, we have to look at how the mind works with the decision-making process. In my book *Trusting Yourself* and on my cassette program *The Prospecting Mentality,* I have talked extensively on this subject, so I will only give a brief overview here.

As I mentioned before, *my contention is that your prospective clients cannot make a decision to buy your product or service unless it feels right to them.* What does it mean to have something "feel right" to you?

### Buying a New Car

Let's say you are getting ready to buy a new car. You want to buy a car that makes logical sense to you and you also want to get a car that feels right to you. Let's say you have a family, so you decide you need a car that has lots of room for people and cargo. Then you want at least a front-wheel drive to get around in the snow. You want a zippy engine so you can pass people when you want to, and you want a comfortable ride.

Now, how do you want to feel when you are driving this car? You have had four-wheel-drive cars before and they have their advantages, but you didn't use the four-wheel drive that much and the maintenance was much higher than on ordinary cars. If you want a more powerful feel, the Jeep Grand Wagoneer with the V-8 would be fun. If you want something rugged but a little more elegant in style, there is the Ford Explorer or the Toyota Four Runner, but they are V-6's. Then you say to yourself, I really don't need four-wheel drive, front-wheel drive is plenty of traction.

Besides, if there is so much snow that I can't get around in a front-wheel-drive car, I should stay home anyway, right? But I do know I want a zippy engine. So now there's the Volvo wagon, which has a turbo, but they are rear-wheel drive. The Saab has a turbo and front-wheel drive, but they are not quite big enough. How about a loaded Taurus wagon? I sure do like the lines on that car, actually a lot more than the four-door coupe. It's got front-wheel drive, plenty of power and pickup, lots of room and comfort. Yes, the Taurus wagon feels right.

Now, what color do you want this car to be? Red would be fun. Red says I'm a sport and have a fun streak in me. It says I am out there a little more. But they say the cops also like to stop red cars more than any other. Dark blue is a rich color, more conservative but more substantial. Then there is white; I have seen some white Taurus station wagons and I really like how they look. There is something regal and pure about a bright white car. Which color am I going to feel the best in, and am I going to feel that way in three years, because I want to keep this car for a while? My suspicion is that white is the color that feels right.

### There's More to It Than Meets the Eye

At this point, I would have to do some test driving and also see how a particular model of car looked in a specific color. I have learned that I like different colors on different cars. So at least we narrowed it down to a Taurus Station Wagon or something very similar based on the qualifying process we just went through.

The point I am illustrating is that having something feel right can be a very elaborate and complicated process. The more options there are, the more choices you have to make. Then you consider the fact that we all have different backgrounds, training, experiences, and different approaches to getting at what feels right. Some people will spend a lot more time on the details, looking at specifications, quality of material and workmanship, consumer reports, and price, to name just a few possibilities. Then there are people on the other end of the spectrum who are much more impulsive. They are usually more concerned about style and how they will be perceived by others when they are driving the car. They will see a car, fall madly in love with that particular car, and then buy it without much more thought. They don't care what other cars are out there or that there might be a smarter or better deal. They have to have that particular car because of how it makes them feel.

I find that no matter what a person's decision-making style happens to be, there are a lot of factors involved in having something feel right or not feel right. Some of the key factors are:

- a vision or sense of what you want
- your values
- your purpose or mission
- your long- and short-term goals
- your overall attitude
- your personality

Generally speaking, the bigger the decision, the more factors involved. The important thing is to realize that people have to go through a process before they know if something feels right to them or not. Your job as a salesperson is to find out where they are in that process. Are they just beginning to gather information, or have they given the idea a lot of thought, as I demonstrated with my car example? The only way you can find out where people are in the process of determining what feels right is to ask questions and listen carefully to their answers.

## THE POWER OF INTUITION

You may have noticed in your own decision-making process or in watching someone else make a decision that you can know whether something feels right or whether it doesn't feel right in a very short amount of time. Sometimes in seconds. You might wonder how this is possible when so much potential information is involved.

### It's Like Riding a Bicycle

The answer to this question is one of the most fascinating phenomena in life. There is a teamwork between different parts of our brain on an ongoing basis to help us learn and make the right decisions toward achieving our goals. Learning to ride a bicycle is one of my favorite examples because it is such an accurate representation of this teamwork. Think back to the time when you learned to ride a bicycle. Maybe you had training wheels, maybe you didn't, but you will remember how the bicycle seemed to lean one way or the other until you learned to balance yourself. Each time you attempted to ride the bicycle the analytical mind would record all the data from those experiences and have them ready for future access.

Another part of the brain, which I call the intuitive mind, had an equally important role. Its job was to take all the information from the analytical mind and turn it into a feeling. It is in this way that you can ride a bicycle today with very little conscious thought. You simply get on the bicycle and remember the feeling of what it is like to successfully balance it. We make it look easy, but the recorded bits and pieces of information required to create the feeling of balancing a bicycle are in the millions when you consider all the different things every body part had to experience in order to learn to balance the bicycle.

Just like the intuitive mind's ability to create the feeling of riding a bicycle, it also has the ability to combine all the important information about who we are — our visions, our values, our goals, our attitudes, and our personality — into a sense of what feels right to us and what doesn't feel right to us. It is as if the intuition can see what actions fit for us and what actions do not. And we have the ability to process all these millions of pieces of information in a few seconds and get a sense of what direction feels right. Unfortunately, we don't always know right away if something feels right to us or it doesn't. Sometimes we *do* know right away. Often we will need more information or more time to process our information before we know what feels right. Or in some cases we may need to relax and get the stress out of the situation before our intuitive direction will become clear. So using our intuition is far from an exact science. It is more of an art. But nevertheless, it is a powerful part of the decision-making process and an extremely effective way to make more of the right decisions in life.

## HOW EMOTION IS DIFFERENT FROM INTUITION

We have been talking about the importance of intuition. Where does emotion fit into the picture? Emotion has traditionally been thought to be the key to making a sale, but I like to make a distinction between emotion and intuition. They are both feelings, so they tend to be lumped together and called "emotion," but upon further examination you will find them distinctly different.

An emotion is a much stronger feeling than intuition. Emotions are anger, sadness, joy, love, hate, etc. Of course emotions are all powerful motivators. Intuition, though, is different in that it is not as intense a feeling as an emotion. An intuitive feeling is very hard to define because each person experiences it a little differently. Some people would call it a "gut feeling," while others would say they know things feel right in their head. Still others will say that they are not sure how to describe it — "they just know" when something feels right. One thing for sure is that an intuitive feeling is very subtle and more difficult to identify than an emotion. I have never had anyone argue the definition of intuition as *a quiet sense of knowing something is right or not right.*

### If the Shoe Fits, Will You Wear It?

Another example of the difference between emotion and intuition is going to the department store to buy a new pair of shoes. You see a pair of shoes that are very interesting looking and the latest fashion. Let's say they are white bucks, and the store is having a 30% off special sale. The salesperson tells you they are selling like hotcakes, that everyone is wearing them. You get excited about being part of the latest thing, being up with the trends, so you buy a pair. You get home and put on your white bucks and they are okay, but you are not totally sure whether you like them as much as you did in the store.

A few days go by and you notice that you are making up excuses not to wear your new shoes. Bottom line — they just don't feel quite right. You felt the emotion of excitement about having a new pair of shoes that were the latest trend, but underneath the emotion was the feeling that they were not quite right for the image you wanted to present to people. So the shoes go back to the store for something else. Your emotions can motivate you to make a decision to buy a pair of shoes. But it is your intuition or whether the shoes feel right or don't feel right that will determine whether you are going to wear the shoes. In other words, emotions will come and go in their intensity, but your intuitive sense of what feels right or doesn't feel right will remain consistent for a longer period of time and will far outlast the consistency of your emotional feelings.

## It Has to Feel Right

What does all this mean in terms of making sales? Emotions are powerful motivators for taking action. Intuitive feelings are just as important and may be more important in the long run in terms of whether your new client is going to keep your product or service. The most important thing is to get your prospective clients to a feeling level in the interview. It doesn't matter if the feeling is emotion or intuition so long as whatever you're proposing "feels right" to your prospective clients. If it feels right, the likelihood of them buying it is extremely strong. On the other side of the coin, if what you are proposing doesn't feel right to your prospective clients in some way, the likelihood of them buying and keeping your product or service is next to none.

In short, if you aren't asking your prospective clients questions that are creating clarity and commitment on a feeling level, they are not going to be able to make a decision when the time comes. They will want to "think about it." Wouldn't you rather have a decision one way or the other?

# Chapter 3

## WHY
## WE
## DON'T
## ASK
## FEELING-ORIENTED
## QUESTIONS

## WHY WE DON'T ASK ...

If finding out what feels right to your prospective clients makes so much sense and is actually required for them to make a buying decision, why do we have such a difficult time asking the feeling-oriented questions?

### Try a Checklist

One reason why we might not ask the feeling-oriented questions is that we simply forget to ask. An easy remedy is to have a *checklist* of the questions you want to ask your prospective clients and make sure you have asked them all before the end of the interview. If you've had some success asking the feeling-oriented questions in the past and you are simply forgetting to ask once in a while, you are in very good shape overall and just need to find a way to remember to ask the questions. Hopefully, this material will convince you beyond any doubt that the key to making more sales is asking the feeling-oriented questions and you will have a much easier time remembering to ask.

### Fear of the Unknown

My experience with the majority of salespeople is that they are not asking the feeling-oriented questions for a variety of more complex reasons. One basic reason people shy away from feeling-oriented questions is that there is an *unknown* element. When you ask a prospective client a feeling-oriented question, there are a lot of possible responses, which makes the answers unpredictable. As you will learn in the discussion that follows, our traditional sales culture values things that are predictable and .controllable, not unpredictable or uncontrollable.

Most salespeople will move away from anything that could complicate the sales process, even though it might increase their overall success in the long run. This kind of thinking is so prevalent in our sales culture that most salespeople will determine that the feeling-oriented questions are not that important and can actually get in the way. This is a fascinating paradox in light of the previous discussion, which says that your prospective clients can't make a buying decision unless your product or service feels right to them. And the way you help them determine what feels right is to help them determine what they want and why they want it.

I have had salespeople say to me: "Now come on, Sid, let me get this straight. I have just spent an hour doing a brilliant job of establishing rapport and my credibility. I have identified some needs. And now you're telling me to risk making my prospective client uncomfortable by asking a dumb question like 'Why is that important to you?' Isn't it obvious why it's important!? If he said he wanted it, why would you need to know anything more?"

My answer is always the same: Because you're missing a lot of sales that you *could* make if you got just a little bit more information.

## THE ROBBER BARON APPROACH

### How It All Got Started

To truly understand why we are a bit nervous asking feeling-oriented questions, we need to look back into history about 100 years to see how our sales culture has evolved. Obviously people have been buying and trading with each other since the beginning of time. But I think you will find that much of our current sales culture has its roots in the industrial revolution. This was a time of radical change. As we moved from an agricultural society to an industrial society, the profession of selling attracted scores of people as more and more products were created that needed to be represented and sold.

If you will take yourself back to history class, you will remember that the industrial revolution had its own set of values. They called the leaders of this age "Kings of Industry" and "Robber Barons." The name of the game was dominance and control, divide and conquer, and they did such a great job that we eventually had to pass laws against forming monopolies. The philosophy of the day was to get the money out of your prospective client's pocket and into yours. In other words, get as much for yourself as possible, and if your client lost out on the deal, that was his problem.

## Making the Sale Was All That Mattered

We are slowly growing out of this long-established way of thinking as we move into the information age, which is also creating a much more sophisticated prospective client. But there are still strong remnants of the industrial revolution in our current sales culture. Because we have valued things like dominance, power, force, and control, is it any wonder that you are considered to have failed if you don't make the sale? The belief has long been that if you were really good, you would masterfully figure out a way to conquer or win over your prospective client and close the sale.

On the other side of the table is the prospective client who has traditionally been seen as the poor soul believed to have no ability to do things for his own good. Therefore he must have the help of a salesperson in order to discover the light and do the right thing, which was always to buy the salesperson's product or service. How the prospective client felt after the sale was something that has long been ignored. If you made the sale, that was the important thing.

So to summarize what I like to call the "Robber Baron" approach to sales, the essence is to dominate and conquer the less-than-sophisticated prospective client into buying our product or service. Considering the prospective client's needs, wants, and goals was not important. The most important thing was to make the sale. Besides, the client is better off with more life insurance (stocks, bonds, whatever) no matter what, right? Buying more life insurance or any other financial product is not the panacea it used to be. Good financial planning is based on doing everything possible to make sure your clients reach their financial goals, not just selling them another product and hoping they make it somehow.

**The Hidden Flaw**

One unfortunate aspect of the Robber Baron approach is that it does work from a narrow perspective. If you regularly call on enough people, and push them into a corner, you will make sales. There always seems to be a fairly large group of prospective clients who think that's just the way it's done. However, this group has grown smaller over the years as people in general are demanding more from the salespeople they buy from.

If I were to say to a Robber Baron salesperson that there is a downside to his approach, he would likely laugh at me and say: "How can there be a downside? I make the sale, I win. End of story." What has become more obvious in recent years is that there is a major flaw in the Robber Baron approach. The flaw is that the approach is based on a win-lose philosophy, which is inherently negative. This philosophy states that the goal is to have the salesperson win by making the sale, and it doesn't matter if the prospective client really benefits or not. The net result of such a negatively-based approach is that there has to be a loss somewhere in the deal. The not-so-obvious aspect of this negatively-based approach is that the salesperson can lose as well as the prospective client, even though the sale was made and commissions were paid.

You might be saying that you can see how the prospective client can lose by being sold something that doesn't really fill his or her needs, but how can the salesperson lose with the Robber Baron approach?

## Robber Barons Pay a Price

One negative aspect that will adversely affect the Robber Baron salesperson is that he may find his new client doesn't like him very much, even though he decided to buy the product or service. The Robber Baron salesperson will often find that if he tries to go back to sell another product, he may not be very welcome. Also, the Robber Baron salesperson will not likely get any referrals, and in many cases, the business won't even stay on the books. Because as soon as the pressure is off from the salesperson, the prospective client will rescind the deal.

Another problem with the Robber Baron approach is that it will burn most people out over time. We need to feel the positive energy and self-esteem that come from genuinely relating to and helping other people. As we become more sensitive to our underlying feelings, we have a tougher and tougher time with the values of the Robber Baron paradigm. The more you care about your prospective clients and whether they get what *they* want, the quicker you will burn out using the old approach. Conversely, the more numb you are to your feelings, the longer you can use Robber Baron techniques before you burn out.

## The Double Bind

Once we notice that something just doesn't feel right about the traditional approach, we start on a quest to discover what does feel right. What we are actually looking for is a combination of self-esteem and self-fulfillment. We want to feel good about ourselves and the work we do at the deepest level. We want to do the right thing for people. We want to feel a surge of energy and sense of pride in the way we do our work. We want to make a positive difference in other people's lives.

When I got into sales, it appeared that you needed to be a driven person who worked very hard and ignored your feelings. Feelings were just distractions that got in the way of doing what had to be done. Furthermore, I was supposed to use any technique (short of illegal) to get people to sign on the dotted line. The most important thing was to make the sale. Now, you're probably saying that you certainly don't fit into the category of a Robber Baron salesperson, and that's good. But it's important to see that much of our sales culture is still operating from the underlying premise of *take the money and run*. The most important thing is to make a good living first. Maybe then you have the luxury to start thinking about really doing the right thing by your client. There is a lot more of this type of thinking around than we would like to admit, and denial of its existence doesn't make it go away.

So if you ever had the feeling that you were not totally comfortable with the way you were taught to sell, this is a common and normal feeling. This feeling of discomfort also tends to get pushed aside very quickly when you get busy trying to survive in a new career and assume you don't know how it's done and listen to those who have been around a while. The pressure to make money can easily cause you to get very numb to your feelings. The fear of not making enough money fast enough can make you toss out a lot of good intentions and drift away from trusting your own instincts about what feels right.

You will start to believe that other people know more than you because they have been around longer and they are making money. You certainly don't want to fail *and* look stupid at the same time. Even though some of the techniques experienced salespeople use may not feel right to you, you assume that they know what they are doing and *you don't*. Before you know it, you are becoming part of the Robber Baron sales paradigm.

## THE DESTRUCTIVE POWER OF FEAR

What holds the Robber Baron paradigm in place? *Fear.* Fear of not making enough sales and therefore not making enough money fast enough. Fear that you can't trust your prospective clients to make a buying decision without pushing them into a corner. Fear that if you don't conquer the prospective client, you won't get paid.

In the short run you can force some sales, get paid, and this approach will appear to work. What isn't often talked about is what happens in the long run to salespeople who are using fear as their primary source of motivation. There is a price to pay for operating from a negative, fear-based context. But the price isn't always very visible at first.

## Redefining Success

We have all heard people say, "You have to define what success means to you." Well, I have been doing just that for many years. It has involved a fair amount of research and my findings have been very surprising.

Success has traditionally been determined by how much money you made. How you did it wasn't considered that important so long as you made the sales. In my work as a peak performance coach over the past 14 years, I have noticed some dramatic shifts in the way people define success. As we get better at telling the truth about what we feel and begin to care more and more about the impact we have on other people, we are looking beyond just making the sale and making lots of money as the sole criteria for success.

Now we consider other key elements, namely our relationship with ourselves or how we feel about our work. Salespeople today want to feel a sense of pride, internal peace, self-esteem, and operate with integrity. It is no longer okay to justify taking advantage of people just because that is the way it's been done for the past 100 years.

There is your relationship with your clients or customers. Salespeople today want to do repeat business. They want to get referrals for a job well done. They want their clients to feel great about what they bought. Salespeople today want to be able to run into their clients at the mall or at the grocery store and enjoy a pleasant conversation, knowing in their hearts they helped them get what they really wanted.

And then there is the subject of health. There is plenty of evidence that ignoring your underlying values of wanting to do the right thing for people can take a serious toll on your health over time. You can't operate from the negative premise of taking advantage of people for your own gain without there being an impact on your physical state of being. Our health and the accidents we have are a mirror of our thinking. Basically, the more fear-based a person's thinking is, the more their behavior will reflect that negative thinking. People usually don't cause accidents on purpose, but by their negative attitude they substantially increase the likelihood of accidents by being more careless and generally less sensitive to potentially dangerous situations.

People operating from a fear-based premise spend a lot of time worrying. Then they tend to put too many unhealthy things in their bodies to numb their worries and deal with the negative stress. Finally the immune system is weakened, and sickness of all kinds becomes more and more frequent.

### The Questions That Don't Often Get Asked

There is no way to predict how a negative, fear-based approach to selling is going to manifest itself, but I guarantee you it will show up somewhere. If a salesperson is making a lot of money using the Robber Baron mentality, you have to ask some more questions that often don't get asked. Questions like:

- Are they keeping the money they are making, or do they seem to lose a lot of what they make from business falling off the books and from poor judgment with their personal finances?

- How do they feel about themselves? Are they happy, or are they simply putting on a happy face while they are feeling miserable underneath?

- Would their clients have positive things to say about them? Would their clients refer them to their friends because they were excited about the service provided?

- How are their relationships with the significant people in their lives? Are they accepting, loving, and empowering toward their immediate family, or are there major communication problems and other conflicts?

- Finally, how much time are they spending in less than ideal health as the result of sickness and accidents?

When you get the answers to these questions, as I have for many years now, you see a clear pattern — and it isn't a positive one. I highly recommend that you reexamine how you have defined success for yourself and look carefully to see if any of your motivation is fear-based. Our careers are challenging enough without adding all the negative complications of being motivated by fear.

## THE CREATIVE POWER OF TRUST

In my coaching practice, I have had many clients who were not aware that there *was* any motivation other than fear. When I have asked these people what would motivate them if we took away the fear, they didn't have an answer. The next question is, what is the opposite of fear?

*Trust.*

Okay, then, what do we put our trust in? Life's basic principles and laws.

## For Every Action There Is a Reaction

There is a law in physics that says for every action there is an equal reaction. If you are putting positive energy out there by the way you approach your work, positive energy is going to come back to you. It can take a little time for the positive energy to come back to you, but it will manifest itself in some positive way in your life. Would you be willing to trust this law?

## We Create Our Own Reality

To a great degree, we create our own reality by the way we react to what happens to us and the attitude we maintain as we go through life. We can choose to be responsible for the thoughts and feelings we have. No one else is to blame for our condition in life. We have made many choices to get where we are today. Sure, there are always some things we can't change, and we can learn to live productively with those circumstances. But there are a lot of things that we *can* change, and our best bet is to trust that making the right choices right now will have the greatest impact on our getting what we really want.

## The Answers Are Within

We each have our own unique answers to the problems and challenges we face in life. These answers are not in a book, seminar, or at a college — they are within ourselves. They are in our thoughts and feelings. We may not be totally aware we have these answers within ourselves, but they are there. And I don't mean to say that other sources of information are not important. We can learn a lot from sources outside our own thoughts and feelings. But when it comes down to making the choices in life that are going to bring the greatest amount of success and happiness, there is one source you can consistently rely on. That is what feels right to you at the deepest level.

## Your Mission, Should You Accept It

The shift to trusting rather than operating from fear is a big change for our sales culture. We have a long way to go but the opportunity is huge. To paraphrase the Chinese proverb: If you want to change the world, you must start with your community. If you want to change your community, you must start with yourself. That is the opportunity we all have — to build momentum on the side of trust rather than on the side of fear in our approach to selling. We have the opportunity as sales professionals to set an example for the business community in general!

*We have the ability, one person at a time, to take our own careers and the whole sales culture to a level of integrity where the prospective client gets what he or she really wants and the salesperson still makes a handsome living. We haven't even begun to tap the power of this approach and the increases in income that are available with this shift in perspective.*

There is a lot of evidence that shifts are occurring in our society and our sales culture. People are choosing to be more aware of underlying feelings that have been ignored for so long. The feeling that we truly *do* care about each other. That we want to get along. That we want to help each other. That we want the other person to prosper as a result of dealing with us. We like the feeling and the results of the "everybody wins" approach as opposed to the more traditional "as long as I win, it doesn't matter who loses" approach. People are realizing that they know what feels right to them and are learning to trust that internal

information and live their lives by it. People in general
expect a lot more from a salesperson. They want the salesperson to help them figure out what their needs are and then
have the technical expertise to get the right solution in
place and make sure it works.

## Old Habits Die Hard

The days of the Robber Baron sales approach are on the
way out, but old habits often die hard. There are still plenty
of people who quietly value control, dominance, and
manipulation and downplay the importance of helping
prospective clients get what *they* want. Basically, you have
to stay very numb and not really care about other people in
order to use the Robber Baron sales approach. The good
news is that if people get in touch with the fact that they
really do care about other people, the Robber Baron
approach gets very uncomfortable. The bad news is that the
Robber Baron approach will be around for as long as there
are people who remain numb to their underlying feelings of
care and concern for others and sell strictly for their own
gain.

I don't put any blame on anyone for the Robber Baron
aspect of our sales culture. I don't blame sales managers or
trainers or home offices. They inherited the Robber Baron
approach like everyone else. That is the way it has been
done for a long time. It also "made sense at the time," like a
lot of things we *used* to do. But once we know better, we
need to make some changes or we will pay for our
indiscretions in ways we never expected.

Underneath the fear that makes us think we have to force
things in order to survive is a heart that cares about people
and a sense of trust in a bigger perspective. We all need to
make the shift away from fear-based motivation and move

toward trust-based motivation for so many reasons: our peace of mind, our mental, physical, and emotional health, and to obtain financial independence — just to name a few.

## Commit to the Bigger Perspective

Helping prospective clients get what they really want is the most powerful shift you can make in your approach to selling. It will bring you self-esteem, a wonderful sense of peace and well-being, a sense of deserving greater financial success, and the validation that you are doing the right thing by discovering that you are making more sales with less struggle and effort.

But there are steps that have to be taken. We have to make the shift to the bigger perspective of caring about whether people get what they really want in their dealings with us. We have to find out what is important to them and why those things are important. We have to make a commitment to helping people make the right decisions based on what *they* feel is right, not solely on what *you* feel is right. Sure, your expertise is important, and some people will want you to tell them what to do. But we can never forget that the decision has to feel right to our prospective clients. We have to trust that our prospective clients know what feels right to them, even if it is different from what we would do for ourselves.

# Chapter 4

## CREATING
## THE
## RIGHT
## ENVIRONMENT
## TO
## ASK
## FEELING
## QUESTIONS

## THE IDEAL RELATIONSHIP

We have talked about why it is so important to ask feeling-oriented questions and why we can have some resistance to asking them. Let's look at how we can make it more comfortable for both you and your prospective clients to get to a feeling level.

### A Partnership

First, let's define the ideal relationship between you and the client. In a word, it should be a *partnership*. It's a team effort. You want your prospective clients to tell you about their wants and needs in relation to your product or service. Then you take those wants and needs and add your expertise and come up with some appropriate recommendations. In the process of making recommendations you educate your prospective clients on the viable options available to solve their problems. From here your job is to help your prospective clients make an informed decision that "feels right" to them because it really fits their overall situation. This is very much a consultative or problem-solving approach.

People love to be interviewed. They love to answer questions, especially if the person asking the questions is genuinely interested in their answers. This means you have to really listen to what people have to say, not just look and act like you're interested. You want to have all your attention focused on getting a clear picture of your prospective client's situation and what potential problems could be solved by your product or service. Notice, I did not say to tell your prospective clients about all the wonderful features and benefits of your product or service. That comes later.

## GETTING THE INTERVIEW STARTED

### Review Your Purpose and Vision

In chapter 10 of my book *Trusting Yourself*, I talk about the importance and power of having a chosen purpose for your business. I state that one of the reasons I like to work with financial services salespeople is their overall desire to establish meaningful relationships with their clients based on mutual trust, rapport, and a sense of friendship. I find that the emotional need to establish meaningful relationships and then help people creatively solve their financial problems and challenges is the driving force (purpose) for a large number of financial services salespeople. However you define your business purpose, reviewing it in your mind is a highly effective way to positively focus all of your energies prior to beginning a sales interview. Get in touch with the feel of your purpose and a vision or feeling for what you would like to accomplish for your next meeting, and you will be consistently rewarded.

I recommend that you keep the vision, goal, or objective of what you want to accomplish in your sales interviews positive and general. Instead of saying "I am going to sell this guy something no matter what," try shifting to a bigger perspective: "I want to have the most positive results possible from this next interview, and I will trust whatever direction the interview takes." The first statement is from the Robber Baron paradigm. The second statement is from a paradigm of trust and faith in the creative process of life.

### General Statement of Benefit

At some point toward the beginning of your sales interview, you are going to need to tell people something about what you are selling or offering. If you don't, you can easily look like you are trying to hide something, which is not a good way to start. Begin by telling people generally what you do that has a clear benefit for the prospective client. The key word here is *general* because you want your opening statement about what you do to be of enough general interest to a large enough group of people that it makes it hard to say no.

For example:

> "What I do is help business owners put more money in their pockets by maximizing their employee benefits."

> "What I do is help people diversify their investment portfolios so that they get the highest possible return with the least risk. Did you know that 94% of the return in a portfolio is determined by the asset allocation?"

Keeping your general statement of benefit brief and to the point is also very important because you want to get your prospective clients involved in the conversation as early as possible.

## Get Permission to Ask Questions

The next step is to *get permission to ask questions.* This is important because it sets up the relationship between you and your prospective clients right from the beginning. You are going to be asking the questions and they are going to be giving you their answers. You want to make it safe and inviting for your prospective clients to want to answer your questions. The best way I know to accomplish this is to get permission to ask questions. You could say:

"So I can best determine what might be of interest to you, would it be okay if I asked you a few questions?"

Or:

"So I can talk more in terms of what might be of interest to you, would it be okay if I asked you a few questions?"

Once someone answers "okay" to this question — and most people will — you have set up the relationship to be the interview*er*. The really great part about this approach is that once you have permission to ask questions, what questions can you ask? Anything you want!

At this point you will have to determine what questions you are the most comfortable with based on your personality style. Some salespeople like to get right to the point, while others like to take more time to establish rapport. You have to develop a sense of what works best for you. As a general guideline, it is usually good to start out with easy questions that have some connection with your product or service. Starting out by asking someone "how they got where they are today" is too general and would take too long to answer. You want to ask questions that will naturally lead into more questions related to the problems you can solve for people. For example:

"Have you done any financial planning?"

"What have you liked about the planning you have done?"

"What have you disliked about the planning you have done?"

"Do you own your home?"

"What other kinds of investments do you like?"

## Focus Your Prospective Clients with a Menu

One approach that I have found very effective in focusing your prospective clients on the topics you want to talk about is to show them a menu of the types of problems you typically solve. This information is usually presented as a list of bulleted items on your letterhead or in a brochure that will take just a minute or two for your prospective clients to read through to see if there is anything they are interested in. The bulleted items need to be solutions to problems that your typical client is likely to have and ideally stated in a way that shows a clear benefit to the pro-spective client.

Menu examples 1 and 3 below are completely done in statements of benefits, whereas menu example 2 is a combination of products sold and problems solved with their corresponding benefits. I don't recommend giving your prospective clients just a list of the products you sell without some corresponding benefits. Your prospective clients won't really know what problems the products are a solution to, and in some cases won't even know what some of the products are. So the more you word the menu in terms of the problems solved and the potential benefits, the more effective the menu will be.

The differences between the three menus shown below are the result of differences in style and of marketing to a variety of prospective clients. All three menus have worked well for different people. You need to create your own menu of benefits related to the problems you want to solve for your prospective clients.

The following are three examples of menus successfully used by my clients:

1.    Investment-Oriented Menu
2.    Personal Life Insurance–Oriented Menu
3.    Business Owner–Oriented Menu

### 1. *Investment-Oriented* Menu

☐ Utilize proven strategies to maximize return on investment and minimize risk.

☐ Tailor your (insurance, investment) plan to best suit your personal short- and long-term needs.

☐ Turn the odds of success in your favor and improve the consistency of your return on investment by diversification.

☐ Save time and avoid mistakes by utilizing the advice of specialists.

☐ Enjoy the "peace of mind" of knowing a well-conceived and safeguarded plan is in place.

☐ Work with advisors who understand and care about your personal objectives and motivations.

☐ Obtain the best protection for your specific liabilities with the life, health, and disability insurance that will give you the most for your money.

## 2. *Personal Life Insurance*–Oriented Menu

### *SAVE MORE MONEY*

( ) MUTUAL FUNDS
( ) ANNUITIES
( ) LIMITED PARTNERSHIPS
( ) IRAs
( ) TAX ADVANTAGED INVESTMENTS
( ) CDs, MONEY MARKET FUNDS

### *INSURE POTENTIAL LIABILITIES*

( ) **COLLEGE FUNDING**
    Guarantees that children will have money for college.
( ) **MORTGAGE FUNDING**
    Pays full mortgage in the event of premature death.
( ) **INSURANCE ANALYSIS**
    Calculates how much life insurance you really need.
( ) **INCOME PROTECTION**
    Guarantees income in the event of disability or sickness.

### *ESTATE TAX PLANNING*

( ) **WILLS**
    Pass assets to proper heirs with maximum tax advantages.
( ) **TRUSTS**
    Maximizing every tax advantage for both you and your heirs.
( ) **LIQUIDITY**
    Protect estate by providing cash to pay for Federal Estate Taxes.

### *FINANCIAL PLANNING*

( ) **WRITTEN FINANCIAL PLAN**
    Identify realistic goals with a plan to achieve them.

### *OTHER CONSIDERATIONS*

( ) **RETIREMENT PLANNING**
    Making sure you have the money you need to retire.
( ) **HEALTH INSURANCE**
    Getting the most for your money.
( ) **LONG-TERM CARE INSURANCE**
    Preserving your estate and dignity in later years.

## 3. *Business Owner–Oriented* Menu

- **Identify additional avenues for reducing taxes** available to you as a business owner.

- **Increase the personal assets of the major owner(s)** or shareholder(s) by better utilizing business assets and cash flow.

- **Provide maximum fringe benefits for owner(s)** or shareholder(s) on a tax-free basis (Medical Reimbursement, Health Insurance, Life Insurance, Disability Income Insurance, Dental Insurance, etc.).

- **Create a plan to protect and maximize business equity** in the event of a major owner's or shareholder(s)' death, disability, or retirement.

- **Assure the proper transfer of assets to heirs** at the death of an owner while minimizing transfer costs (taxes) by using advanced planning techniques.

- **Encourage employee longevity by developing a pension plan for employees** with minimal cost to the business.

- **Selectively compensate major owner(s) or key people** by designing a plan that allows for discrimination.

- **Secure the most efficient pension plan possible** for your business by reviewing the qualified plan alternatives and determining which option best fits your long-term objectives (SEP, IRA, Profit Sharing, 401K, Money Purchase, Defined Benefit, Keogh, etc.).

Once you have a menu you are comfortable with, simply put it in front of your prospective client when the time feels right toward the beginning of the interview. Ask him or her to read through the menu and see if there is anything there that might be of potential interest. This is a piece you can leave behind, so it should look professional.

Also, I have found that if you don't number each menu item, it makes your prospective clients have to describe in words what is of interest to them. When I have numbered each menu item, prospective clients tended to say "Number 2 is of interest," rather than telling me in *words* what was of interest to them. I stopped numbering menu items for this reason.

## ESTABLISHING RAPPORT

### Having Something in Common

Your goal in the early part of an interview is to keep your prospective clients interested and begin to establish rapport. You will keep their interest if they feel the questions are going somewhere and you are demonstrating that you care about them by listening to their answers. You will establish rapport by uncovering things you have in common. That actually is the definition of rapport: *having something in common*. The more you have in common, the deeper the level of rapport.

There are lots of things you may have in common with your prospective clients:

- where you are from
- where you went to school
- where you live now
- your interests

- your values
- your hobbies
- your generation or approximate age
- your life experiences

The list is endless. The skill is to identify things that you have in common with your prospective clients and let them know about it.

Try to find things in common with your prospective clients as soon as possible in the interview. Often you can find things you have in common by being observant when you walk into your prospective client's office or home. You can also find things in common during the "small talk" that usually begins most meetings. If you don't have time for small talk or your style is to get to the point, then you have to look for things in common during the interview and be sure to take a minute or two to talk about anything you notice you have in common, even though it may seem off the subject. You can always go back to whatever you were talking about — and you will resume your fact-finding at a deeper level of rapport.

## Nonverbal Rapport

There are also a variety of *nonverbal* methods for speeding up the rapport-building process. Remember, anything you have in common with another person will build rapport so long as they are open to being in rapport with *you*. Some nonverbal things you can match or mirror with your prospective clients are: body posture, gestures, facial expressions, movements, speed of speech, and tone of voice, to name a few of the obvious ones. I find that nonverbal rapport happens quite naturally, and I don't place much conscious attention on it. If you are going to consciously match or mirror other people's behavior in any way, make sure it feels right to do so and that you keep your focus on helping your prospective clients get what *they* really want.

## The Power of Shared Experience

I have spent many hours studying and experimenting with rapport-building skills, but I still find that the most powerful rapport builder is listening and letting people know that you are listening. You might be wondering how listening can create something in common with your prospective client. It is obvious once you hear it. You are actually sharing an experience together. You are both sharing the experience of the questions you are asking and your prospective clients' answers. And sharing an experience with your prospective clients is extremely powerful in terms of rapport building.

Think back through your life. Who are the people you feel closest to regardless of how often you actually spend time together? My bet is that you shared at least one intensely emotional experience together, maybe several, or maybe even many. These experiences can include things like taking a risk together; winning together; losing together; making it through a tough situation together; having a disagreement, resolving it, and becoming friends; or any other situation or circumstance where you shared an intense feeling or emotion with another person.

Obviously a sales interview is usually not going to take on the intensity level of the examples I have just given, but you can easily move in the direction of shared experience and a deepened level of rapport if you get to a feeling level in your conversation.

## LETTING THEM KNOW YOU CARE

### Really Listening

Letting people know that you are listening is also a very powerful rapport builder, and there are several ways to accomplish this. To really listen and hear what others are saying is an exercise in patience and trust — patience while you are listening to what others have to say, and trust that you will have something intelligent to say when they stop talking. Most of us tend to listen until something is said that reminds us of a similar experience or our own thoughts and feelings on the subject, and then we want to talk. Usually we don't listen very well after we realize we would like to share our own experience about whatever is being talked about by the other person. This is why most of us are starving to be listened to because very few people really listen to us for very long before they are thinking about themselves. Most people are focusing their attention on what they are going to say as soon as you pause to take a breath.

It is fairly easy to become someone who people will not soon forget by simply focusing more on your listening. I have found that really listening to another person is much more powerful in building rapport than anything I might have to say. What I mean by listening is a lot more than maintaining eye contact and nodding your head occasionally while you monitor your own judgments about what is being said and think about what you want to say.

Listening to your prospective clients should involve every part of your mind, body, and soul. You totally yet *lightly* focus on the other person. You quiet the judgments of your internal critic. You are alert yet relaxed, taking in every nuance, every inflection, every emotion, every sound, every word. You have no concern about what you are going to say next. You trust that when it is time for you to talk, something appropriate or fitting will occur to you without effort. At the same time, you are aware of what you feel, sense, see, and hear inside yourself as you remain focused on totally absorbing what the other person is communicating. A friend of mine describes listening as being able to become aware of everything others are communicating by what they say, what it sounds like when they say it, what they look like when they say it, and what you feel when they say it.

Listening in this way takes all your attention, but it does not take effort as much as a relaxed focus. You will take in a lot of information on both conscious and subconscious levels. Your mind will naturally sort out what's important and what isn't during the conversation if you stay relaxed and open. You will get the specifics of what is being said along with the "bigger picture" of the other person's attitude and intent. And you'll find that you will still have lots of things to say to people even if you stop thinking about what you are going to say beforehand.

## Being Nonjudgmental

Being nonjudgmental when you are interviewing someone is extremely powerful because it creates a safe environment for your prospective client to talk. We have all been in at least a few situations where we innocently shared what we felt and then were brutally criticized or even ridiculed. Imagine what it would be like to have a conversation with someone and know that you won't be judged in any way, that you can't make a mistake, that you can't mess up, and that you can't say the wrong thing. I guarantee you that if you create that kind of environment for the people you interview, you are going to make a lot of friends as well as a lot of sales. People are starving for the opportunity to talk about themselves in a safe environment. If you demonstrate that you are not going to judge people in any way, they will tell you everything you want to know and more.

One of my favorite memories from my early days in the life insurance business was calling on a crusty gas station owner. We eventually got around to talking about life insurance, and he told me that he wanted some of that "term insurance with the cash value." My immediate impulse was to show off how much I knew and correct him by telling him that term insurance doesn't have cash value. But instead I caught myself, thought for a second, smiled and said, "We can get you some of that." He smiled back at me and said, "Good. What do you need from me?"

**Repeating Your Prospective Client's Exact Words**

Repeating back other people's exact words instead of using your own words is another powerful rapport builder. Even though two people speak the same language in general terms doesn't mean that they would use the same words to describe the same situation. If you take five people who all witnessed a car crash followed by an explosion and you ask them all to describe what they saw, you are going to get a wide variety of words used to describe the same event. We are all actually speaking a little different language because we all have different backgrounds, training, and life experiences. Furthermore, whatever words people use to describe something can have a lot of meaning to them. There can be many hundreds, even thousands, of pieces of information attached to the meaning of a single word. So if you change the words your prospective clients use and use your own, it is not likely to have the same meaning and you will have lost a level of rapport.

Early in my sales career I had the habit of changing the words that other people would use to describe what they wanted and using my own words. My words made more sense to me, so I figured they would make more sense to my prospective clients. The problem was that *I* understood better what I was talking about, but they didn't know what I meant by the words I was using. I could clearly feel that I was taking something away from our rapport when I would repeat back my words rather than theirs. Then one day I stumbled onto the idea of using other people's words exactly as they said them — and the difference was phenomenal.

Remember Gene, the father from Chapter One? Remember why he wanted to buy life insurance? He said he wanted to guarantee that his children would have the money to go to college no matter what happened. He said he felt that he had struggled financially because he couldn't go to college and he didn't want his children to have to struggle as he did. Furthermore, he said life is hard enough without having disadvantages and he wanted to give his children every advantage possible to get good jobs.

If you were repeating back to Gene what he had said to you, do you think it would be as powerful to summarize in your own words and say, "Gene, it sounds to me like you want your children to go to college so they can make a lot of money"? What is Gene going to say at this point? He is probably in a state of shock, but let's say he keeps his composure and says something like "Well, that isn't exactly what I said but it's in the ballpark." Do you think that Gene might question whether you knew what he wanted at this point? You bet. Gene risked telling you exactly what he wanted and why he wanted it, and then you repackaged it in your own words and it came out all wrong. Use your prospective clients' exact words to describe things that are important to them and you will eliminate a lot of potential miscommunication.

## Draw People Out

It is also important to make sure we understand the meaning of what others say to us and *not assume we know what they said*. A corollary to "using other people's words" is to *draw people out* by getting them to explain in more detail what they mean. If you get people talking in more detail about what they want, they will define it in more detail for themselves, which makes it more real and eventually easier to buy your product if it helps them get what they want.

It is important to be *inviting and encouraging* so that your prospective clients want to work a little harder at explaining their thoughts and feelings. The following six sample questions are designed to get people to explain what they have said in greater detail.

"Can you tell me a little more about that?"

"Can you say more about that so I have a better sense of what you mean?"

"Say more about that ..."

"Tell me more about that ..."

"Can you describe that a little more for me?"

"How would you know if you had that? What would it be like?"

## Turn a Statement into a Question

Turning a statement into a question is another powerful way to let your prospective clients know you care about what they think and feel. Remember, when you are telling someone something, they can ignore it, judge it, or not even hear what you are saying because they are thinking about something else. But when you ask someone a question, the spotlight is on them and they have to engage and be involved in the conversation. Also, turning a statement into a question is an excellent way to put stronger emphasis on a point and still end up asking your prospective clients for their input.

For example:

> "Despite all the press for 'buy term and invest the difference,' it has been shown that permanent insurance is a better long-run solution if you have a long-term insurable need. How do *you* feel about that?"

## Taking Notes

I have always been big on taking notes when people talk to me. I'm not talking about writing down every word. That can actually discourage people from talking. But you *can* write down key words. Even with a few words on a page of note paper, you will remember the conversation a lot better when it's time to prepare for your next conversation. You will also find that when you get to a feeling level with your prospective clients, they are often sharing information with you that they may have never told anyone else. You don't want to take this information lightly. You want to remember it. And if you are seeing lots of people, it can become difficult to remember the key information without some notes.

I have a friend who doesn't feel comfortable taking notes in the initial interview. He wants to go in and "just be" with the person during the initial interview. Then, when he gets back to his car, he dictates everything he can remember about the conversation. However you do it, get the important information written down somewhere so you can review it before you talk again. The experience of having someone remember that what you said was important to you is priceless. You will remember that person because he demonstrated that he was listening and valued what you said as important. Don't miss the opportunity to be remembered by the people you talk to in this same way.

## Trusting Your Instincts

Trusting your instincts during your interviews with prospective clients is a subtle yet highly effective way to get magical results. People often ask me how they can speed up the process of having someone else trust them. My answer is often simply to *trust yourself*. What this means is, be willing to listen to your internal voice and feelings when you are in an interview and be willing to trust and act on what your senses tell you to do. If you get the thought to ask a different question than the one you usually ask, ask the new one. If you get the feeling that your prospective client's attention is somewhere else, don't keep going with the interview. Stop and ask if this is a good time to talk. The magical thing that happens with other people when you trust your intuitive instincts is that they experience you as being more tuned in to them than most other people. This creates a powerful sense of rapport and trust on a conscious and a subconscious level because people start to feel that you are really listening and paying attention. This is much more attention than they usually get, and they will remember you for it.

## "Get on Their Side of the Table"

One of the most powerful things you can do to develop trust and rapport with your prospective clients is to "get on their side of the table." See the world as they see it. Go with the flow of how they answer your questions. Don't disagree or argue in any way with what they say. I like to go as far as to say, always give your prospective clients "a way out." If you feel like you need to back people into a corner in order to make the sale, there is some fear sneaking back into the picture. Pushing people to do or say things out of a fear that you won't make the sale if you don't push creates a negative context and has to produce negative results somewhere. We don't know exactly how the negative results will manifest, but they will. You have to trust that plenty of people are still going to buy if you trust them to reach their own conclusions. My research points in only one direction: *The more respect you show your prospective clients by helping them discover what they really want, the more they buy.* Not only do they buy more often, but you get to feel great because you helped them make what they feel is the right decision. You won't have to worry about whether that kind of business stays on the books, and you'll find yourself getting a lot more referrals from satisfied clients!

## BEING LIKABLE

How much time do you spend with people who make you uncomfortable? As little as possible, right? You figure out a way to politely excuse yourself as quickly as you can. So being as likable as possible will be to your advantage.

Create an inventory of how to be likable and what to avoid in order to stay out of the unlikable category by trusting your experience. Think of three people you know and like and write down the things you like about them. Pay special attention to what they do that makes you feel good about yourself. Then take the other side and think of three people who make you uncomfortable and determine what they do that makes you feel that way. This will give you a good starting list.

Be sure that you reword the qualities of what you want to avoid into their positive counterpart. For example, in the past I have had a tendency to talk too fast. It wouldn't be as effective for me to be saying to myself, "Don't talk too fast," as it would be to remind myself to "take my time." With negative commands like "Don't talk too fast," the mind has to create an image of the thing you don't want to do first and then try to think in terms of not doing it. It is much simpler to think in terms of the positive command of "take your time."

Daily reviewing the qualities you want to have is one of the most powerful warmups I know for getting your day off to a great start. It also does wonders for your confidence and your ability to influence others when you can feel and know that you are a combination of many wonderful positive qualities.

I have developed a list of qualities that I have found develop strong positive feelings when reviewed on a regular basis. Because everyone attaches slightly different meanings and feelings to different words, you may want to add or subtract from the list below. Look for those words that hook your most positive feelings. Whether you review five words or fifty, find the words and phrases that have the most meaning and feeling for you. Review them regularly and you will charge out the front door in the morning!

When you internalize your sense of these qualities, you will come across as very likable to the people you interact with.

Think of what it would feel like to possess the following qualities as powerfully as you can imagine.

| | |
|---|---|
| confident | integrated |
| tenaciously positive | powerful |
| versatile | balanced |
| decisive | practical |
| disciplined | effective |
| solution-oriented | logical |
| fearless | articulate |
| fun-loving | empathetic |
| feeling | sensitive |
| highly productive | intuitive |
| forgiving | loving |
| caring | open |
| vulnerable | trusting |
| emotionally mature | positive |
| committed | inspiring |
| magical | kindhearted |
| warm | gentle |
| financially independent | viable |
| patient | graceful |
| elegant | artful |
| impactful | healthy |
| profitable | peaceful |

## CHEMISTRY AND TIMING

It is also important to know that you can do *too much* to accommodate a prospective client. If you feel good about who you are being and you don't establish a sense of rapport and trust with someone fairly quickly, there is likely something major in the way of forming a workable relationship. Yes, there is the possibility that you could resolve whatever was "in the way" over time if you wanted to put in the effort. But there is even greater evidence that whatever is not working about the relationship in the beginning will always be a problem in one way or another. In my cassette tape program *The Prospecting Mentality*, I refer to this phenomenon as *chemistry and timing*.

My *Chemistry and Timing Formula* has doubled so many incomes it is worth repeating the basic concepts here. First, having *chemistry* with someone else means that there is a basic affinity and desire to want to continue the relationship. *Timing* simply means that your prospective client has a need for your product or service at this time.

The question is, *Have you ever sold a case where there wasn't chemistry and timing?*

Most salespeople today will answer this question with a "no." So if you spend some time with a prospective client and determine the chemistry just isn't there, you should move on. If the chemistry *is* there and the timing isn't, you simply put that prospective client's card back in your tickler file for a later call.

When I first discovered the Chemistry and Timing Formula, I was working with a financial planner who was taking 150 prospective clients a year through a four-interview process, and about one-third of the people were actually buying something. One day I happened to ask the financial planner if he ever got a sense of who was going to buy something and who wasn't. He said that actually he did get a sense and his perception was accurate most of the time. I asked him at what point in the process he had this sense. He said the first interview.

So I said, "Let me make sure I understand. You have a sense of who is going to buy and who isn't in the first interview, and you are right most of the time?" He said, "Yes, I guess that's right." Then I said, "So if you know who is going to buy and who isn't in the first interview, why would you take the other 100 people through a four-interview process?" His answer is typical of the way we have all been trained to think. He said, "I wouldn't want to miss anyone who might change their mind." Two-thirds of his efforts (400 interviews) were focused on people he knew would likely not buy anything, yet he pursued them with the hope that some of them might change their minds!

Needless to say, I saw an opportunity here. I talked the financial planner into working only with the people he had a sense were going to do something and not pursuing the others for a test period of one year. Guess what happened? He more than doubled his income and worked a lot fewer hours. Since discovering the Chemistry and Timing Formula, I have had hundreds of clients adopt this approach with equally outstanding success.

It takes some courage to walk away from business you could probably close if you went back enough times. But if you were to talk to my clients who swear by this formula, they all say the same thing. Chasing "china eggs," rather than finding prospective clients who they get along with and who want to do something, was costing them dearly in terms of income and self-esteem. Dump the china eggs, dump anyone you don't feel some chemistry with, regardless of their net worth. Your income, your self-esteem, and the amount of fun you have with your business will all take an instant quantum leap!

# *Chapter 5*

# GETTING
# TO
# THE
# FEELING
# LEVEL

## DIFFERENT LEVELS OF COMMUNICATION

There are different levels of communication that move from simple to complex and from impersonal to personal. The most basic level of communication is talking about *things,* such as the weather, places, events, or circumstances. These are easy and accepted subjects that are the source of most "small talk." The next level is talking about *people.* This is a topic of great interest to most people and a bit more complex than the first level. The third level is talking about *ideas,* which are usually more complex but often less personal. And then finally we get to sharing *feelings,* which are the most personal level of communication and can also be very complex in meaning.

The important thing to notice is that in conversation, most people will tend to start out with the more simple and less personal levels of communication and then move to the more complex and more personal levels. That is why you want to start your interviews with easy questions to get people talking, give some time to establish rapport, demonstrate that you are a "safe" person to talk to, and then eventually get around to asking the feeling-oriented questions.

Most people will tend to give you information from the first three levels of communication before they will get to their feelings. However, there is a group of people who are very comfortable expressing their feelings very quickly. When you are talking to this "expressive-style" personality, they will often give you so much feeling information that it may take some time to sort it all out. The challenge in this case is to determine which feelings are most important. The good news is that this personality style is easy to identify and easy to work with in terms of finding out what is really important to them. Since the expressive-style personality is only about 10% of the population, you will find that most of the time the challenge in your interviews is going to be getting people to express themselves at a feeling level.

## WHY IS THE FEELING LEVEL THE MOST COMPLEX?

The feeling level is the deepest and most complex level of communication because of how our brains process information. I have gone into this subject in detail in my book *Trusting Yourself,* so I will simply summarize here. The bottom line is that we can process millions of pieces of information per second with our feelings. At the same time, this amazing ability creates a potential problem. Since we can process so much information with our right brain in the form of intuition and emotion, there is no way for us to consciously monitor how we arrive at our feeling conclusions or how we feel about something. With the left brain's sequential, linear processing, it is easy to consciously monitor how we arrive at conclusions. This creates a much greater sense of confidence about what we have "figured out," as opposed to the risk of acting on an "intuitive hunch" with no proof that it will work.

As I mentioned earlier, we have all had the experience of sharing feelings and then being criticized or ridiculed for what we said. We may have been told we were crazy or stupid or bad. Whatever the negative communication was, we quickly learned that it isn't very smart to share our feelings without some confidence that we will be well received no matter what we say. So sharing feelings can be dangerous because they are so easily misunderstood and negatively judged by whomever we are sharing our feelings with. Most of us have naturally developed the tendency to speak in terms of what we think the other person is going to understand and accept. We will save sharing our feelings openly for people we can trust to have a genuine respect for whatever we feel or think. For most of us, this is a small group. Therefore, if you create this level of safety for your prospective clients when you are with them, you are going to find yourself in greater and greater demand as an advisor. People are starving for advisors they can really talk to so they can get at what they really want. Would you want it any other way for yourself?

Furthermore, it is my contention that people will not buy your product or service unless they are clear that whatever you are presenting feels intuitively right to them. What "intuitively right" means is that it fits their vision of what they want to create in the long term combined with their most deeply held values. The best way I know to find out what feels intuitively right to prospective clients is to ask them, and the only questions that are going to get the answers at the feeling level are the feeling-oriented questions.

## HOW DO WE RECOGNIZE A FEELING-LEVEL RESPONSE?

One example of a way to help us recognize a feeling-level response is to ask ourselves, Why do people buy life insurance? They buy for reasons like:

- fear of loss
- a greater sense of security
- a greater peace of mind
- love
- an obligation to provide for certain people
- a sense of responsibility toward certain people in their lives

All of these "reasons" are also feelings. We have to be able to help our prospective clients get clear about their feelings

and recognize when we have gotten a feeling-level response. The main criterion for determining if you are
getting a feeling-level response from your prospective
clients is simply to ask yourself, Is their response something they can feel?

You can feel a fear of loss. If people say to you they are
buying life insurance because they have seen the hardship
that can occur from premature death in their own family
and they don't want to put that burden on their immediate
family, that's a feeling-level response. They have a firsthand experience. This is something they have feelings
about. Likewise, you can feel a sense of security or greater
peace of mind. Or, when someone loves his or her family,
he or she feels obligated and responsible to provide for
them. These are all things your prospective clients can feel.

The general rule is, if you ask your prospective clients why
something is important to them and you get a response that
has something in it they can feel, you are on the right track.
If you are not sure whether their response is something they
can feel, you are probably not there yet.

## HOW DO WE GET TO A FEELING LEVEL?

What follows on the next few pages are several scenarios
designed to show you some examples of questions you can
use to get to a feeling level. What I have presented is very
specific, and you can use it exactly as is. But please don't
get the idea that these are the only questions you can use to
get to a feeling level. As you are reading through the
scenarios, ask yourself what questions you would ask in the
same situation. Remember, the most important thing is to
get your prospective clients to a feeling level one way or
another. Also remember, you won't have to ask all of these
questions of people who readily share on a feeling level.

The questions presented in this chapter are more for the people who need a nudge to get to a feeling level.

You can ask a feeling question like the example below with "You" being the salesperson and "John" being the prospective client.

*You*:    "How do you feel about the life insurance you own?"

*John*:    "I feel good about it. I like the peace of mind and feeling of security that it gives me."

This reply has lots of feeling. John feels "good," feels "peace of mind," and feels a "sense of security" about owning life insurance. Unfortunately, it is usually not that simple. Most often your prospective client will give you something other than how he or she feels. For example:

*You*:    "How do you feel about the life insurance you own?"

*John*:    "Oh, I think it's a good idea."

There is nothing in this response that your prospective client can feel in this example. You really know nothing about how John feels. What do you do?

There is a simple solution. Basically, you have to *ask more questions* until you get to a feeling-level response. More specifically, you take the answers your prospective clients give you, and you say that a lot of people have said the same thing, but you want to know why *they* feel that way. This makes total sense to your prospective clients because a lot of different people say the same thing. It is logical that different people are going to have different reasons for saying the same thing. I call this the "**Why is that impor-tant to _YOU_**" approach. For example:

_You_:    "How do you feel about the life insurance you own?"

_John_:   "Oh, I think it's a good idea."

_You_:    "You know, many people have told me the same thing, but let me ask you, why do _you_ think it's a good idea?"

_John_:   "Well, I think it's important to provide a cushion for my family in case I don't live as long as I plan to."

This is good. This would be plenty of feeling-oriented in-formation for most salespeople. However, you can still take it to another level.

_You_:    "How do you feel about the life insurance you own?"

_John_:   "Oh, I think it's a good idea."

_You_:    "You know, many people have told me the same thing, but let me ask you, why do _you_ think it's a good idea?"

_John_:   "Well, I think it's important to provide a cushion for my family in case I don't live as long as I plan to."

_You_:    "Again, John, I've had a lot of people tell me that they wanted to provide a cushion for their family. Why would that be important to _you_?"

*John*:    (Thinks for a few seconds and then replies) "I care about my family and if something were to happen to me, I would want them to feel like I did my best to provide for them."

What is John really saying here? First, that he loves his family and he wants them to feel good about him as a provider. Now we're really getting somewhere. Can you feel the difference?

A lot of wonderful things are happening here. John is getting very clear about why he owns life insurance (and may be thinking that having some more would be a good idea). *You* are clear about why John owns life insurance. You have created a safe environment for John to share his feelings, which he deeply appreciates. Your relationship with John has gone to a much deeper level because he has shared how he feels with you. With just a couple of questions, you have achieved 80% of what needs to happen to have a new client! (The other 20% is the features and benefits of the product and the technical discussion.)

## HELPING PROSPECTIVE CLIENTS VISUALIZE WHAT'S IMPORTANT TO THEM

One of the key premises of creating anything in life is that it works best to have a target to aim at. For some this is best done with a *vision,* but for those people who find it difficult to visualize, a *target feeling* of how you want to feel works just as well.

The power of creating a target vision or target feeling is that it creates something for your prospective clients to have a feeling about. Below is a conversation between *You* and *John* well into your interview. As each question is asked, it helps John get clearer about what he really wants.

*You*:      "John, of the different things we have discussed today, **what** would you say **is most important?**"

*John*:    "I think that retirement planning is probably most important."

*You*:      "You know, John, retirement planning is important to a lot of people these days. **Why is that important to *YOU*** at this point?"

*John*:    "Well, I have a concern that if we don't do some planning, time will slip away and we won't be ready when it's time to retire."

*You*:      (**Long Run Question**) "John, let's say that you and I do some planning so that you *are* ready when it's time to retire. **How will that help you in the long run?**"

*John*:    "Well, if I have a plan in place, there is going to be a much greater likelihood that I am going to succeed at reaching my goals and enjoy my retirement. And I think if I have a plan in place, I am going to feel more at ease about the whole thing."

*You*:      (**Summary Question**) "If you and I could do some retirement planning so that you are *ready when retirement time arrives*, so that you have the *greatest likelihood of reaching your goals* and *enjoying your retirement,* and probably most important, *feel more at ease about the whole thing,* **is that what you want?**"

*John*:    "Yes."

*You*:      "John, what we need to do next is …"

What you don't see with these questions in written form is that when you ask these questions of John, he has to stop and think about his answers. Especially with the **Long Run Question**, John has to project himself into the future and determine how doing some retirement planning now is going to help him in the future. If you can get your prospective clients to imagine the benefits of your service in the future, it makes the benefits a lot more real and a lot easier to buy.

Notice that all the way through the conversation, I was careful to use John's exact words as much as possible about what he said he wanted. As we discussed previously, we don't want to risk using words that may have different meanings at such a crucial point in the interview.

The sequence of questions was:

1. **What's most important?**
2. **Why is that important to *YOU*?**
3. The **Long Run Question**: Summarize his answers from question (1) and question (2), then ask: "How will that help you in the long run?"
4. The **Summary Question:** Summarize all answers and ask: "Is that what you want?"

If this looks or sounds complicated, don't be fooled. The questions flow right together, and with a little practice you will have enough confidence to give these questions a try.

**Very important**: Role-play with a friend until you have the feel for the flow of the questions.

If all you do is ask your prospective clients **what is important** and **why** *that* **is important to** *them*, you have asked more feeling-oriented questions than most salespeople. So don't feel like you need to ask all the questions being presented or do it in the exact order being presented. The most important thing is to be familiar with what it feels like and sounds like to get your prospective clients to a feeling level and to be able to recognize feeling-oriented answers when you hear them.

## GETTING TO AN EVEN DEEPER FEELING LEVEL

Let's change the scenario a little and get to an even deeper feeling level with John. Instead of asking how retirement planning would help John in the long run, I am going to ask him what he wants to do when he retires. I am going to get him to expand on what he wants to do, so we have identified some specific items. Then I am going to ask him if he can get a sense of what it would be like to be able to retire and do those things. As soon as I ask this question, John is going to imagine what it would be like to retire and do the things he mentioned. Then I am going to ask him if that is an important feeling for him to have. I am getting John to get specific about what he wants and get a sense of what it would be like to have it. I am getting him to visualize and feel what it would be like to have what he wants.

*You*:    "John, of the different things we have discussed today, **what** would you say **is most important**?"

*John*:   "I think that retirement planning is probably most important."

*You*:    "You know, John, retirement planning is important to a lot of people these days. **Why is that important to *YOU*** at this point?"

*John*:   "Well, I have a concern that if we don't do some planning, time will slip away and we won't be ready when it's time to retire."

*You*:   "John, let me ask you: **What do you want to be able to do when you retire?**"

*John*:   "Oh, I don't know. I guess I want to be able to have the time and money to do the things I enjoy doing."

*You*:   "**What do you enjoy doing?**"

*John*:   "Oh, play some golf, travel a little, spend some time with the grandkids, that kind of thing."

*You*:   "**Can you get a *sense* of what it would be like** to retire and do the things you want to do, like play golf, travel, and spend some time with the grandkids?"

*John*:   "Sure."

*You*:   "**Is that an important feeling for you to have?**"

*John*:   "Yes."

*You*:   "John, I can help you get there. What we need to do next is ..."

The same objectives are accomplished in this conversation, except we went to a deeper feeling level. We got John to talk more specifically about what he wants to do when he retires. We got him to get a *sense* of what it would be like to be able to do those things he wants to do (feeling level). And we asked him if that would be an important feeling for him to have (pointed him back to the vision and feeling of what he wanted).

The sequence of questions was:

1. **What's most important?**
2. **Why is that important to *YOU*?**
3. **Draw out specifics:**
   "What do you want to be able to do when you retire?"
   "What do you enjoy doing?"
4. **Feeling Question to make it real:**
   "Can you get a sense of what it would be like ...?"
5. **Feeling Question for commitment:**
   "Is that an important feeling for you to have?"


## DISABILITY EXAMPLE

*You*:    "Fred, we've been talking about your life insurance and your disability coverage today. **What** would you say **is most important** at this point?"

*Fred*:    "I think that disability insurance is probably most important."

*You*:    "Disability insurance is important to most people these days. **Why would you say it's important to *YOU*?**"

*Fred*:    "I think it's important to protect your earning power against getting sick or injured."

*You*:    "**And why would *that* be important** to you, Fred?"

*Fred*:    "Because my expenses don't stop if I can't work."

*You*: "Let me ask you another question so I am sure I understand. **Why would it be important to have your expenses paid if you were sick or injured?**"

*Fred*: "Because I don't want anyone to have to take care of me. I just don't feel that would be right."

*You*: "**Can you get a sense of what it would be like to have** this coverage in place so you would not have to worry about anyone ever having to take care of you if you couldn't work?"

*Fred*: "Yes, I can imagine that."

*You*: "**Is that an important feeling for you to have?**"

*Fred*: "Yes."

*You*: "Here are a couple of options available for this kind of coverage ..."

Notice in this scenario that when I asked Fred why disability insurance was important to him, I didn't get a feeling-level answer. He said it's important to protect your earning power. So then I asked him why *that* would be important, and he said it was because his expenses didn't stop if he couldn't work. This is also not a feeling answer, so I asked him again why it would be important to have his expenses paid if he were sick or injured. Finally we got to a feeling-oriented response. He said he didn't want anyone to have to take care of him. That it just didn't feel right.

Hopefully you are starting to sense where you stop with logical answers instead of going for a feeling-level response from your prospective client.

The sequence of questions was:

1. **What's most important?**
2. **Why is that important to *YOU*?**
3. **Why would *THAT* be important?**
4. **Why would *THAT* be important?**
5. **Feeling Question to make it real:**
   "Can you get a sense of what it would be like to have ...?"
6. **Feeling Question for commitment:**
   "Is that an important feeling for you to have?"

## ESTATE TAX EXAMPLE

*You*:    "Jerry, you told me you're worth $3.5 million and you have a wife and three children. As we have discussed, the estate tax that will have to be paid to the government when you and your wife are gone is about $1.2 million. **What would be most important** in terms of what you want to have happen when you die?"

*Jerry*:    "First of all, I want to pay the least amount of estate taxes possible."

*You*:    "You know, Jerry, a lot of people tell me they want to pay the least amount of estate taxes possible. **Why is that important to *YOU*?**"

*Jerry*:    "I want as much money as possible to go to my family."

*You*:    "If you didn't do anything to minimize the estate taxes, your family would get a fair amount of money as it is. **Why is it important** for them to get as much as possible?"

*Jerry*:    "That's an interesting question. Some people are afraid of spoiling their children with too much money. But I don't think that money ruins people as much as the lack of proper values. My kids have already shown me that they have the values to handle money responsibly. But probably most important, having money gives you the opportunity to bend life to fit your dreams. I want my kids to have that opportunity."

*You*:    "**Let's look into the future** and say that you're gone, but you and I were able to do the planning that allowed you to minimize your estate taxes and give your wife and children as much money as possible. Most important, they have the money they need to bend life to fit their dreams. **How would that make you feel?**"

*Jerry*:    "That would give me great peace of mind knowing that my family was taken care of."

*You*:    "**Is that an important feeling for you to have?**"

*Jerry*:    "Yes, I see what you're getting at."

*You*:    "Good. What we need to do next is ..."

I repeated back to Jerry the facts of the situation, which were his net worth, that he had a wife and three children, and that his approximate estate taxes would be $1.2 million. Then I asked him what would be most important when he died. After he said that he wanted to pay as little tax as possible, I wanted to know why he felt that way. Jerry had some very specific ideas about how he felt toward his kids.

So I projected Jerry into the future, summarized what he said he wanted, and then asked how it would make him feel to have everything he said he wanted. Then I asked him if that were an important feeling to have to confirm his commitment.

The sequence of questions was:

1. **What is most important?**
   "Why is that important to *YOU?*"
2. **Why is *that* important?**
   "Why is it important for them to get as much (money) as possible?"
3. **Project into the future:**
   "Let's look into the future and say you're gone ..."
4. **Feeling Question to make it real:**
   "How would that make you feel?"
5. **Feeling Question for commitment**:
   "Is that an important feeling for you to have?"


## INVESTMENT EXAMPLE

*You*:    "Jane, I know you were referred by the Johnsons, who have been clients of mine for years. But tell me, what brings you here today?"

*Jane*:   "Actually, my grandfather passed away several months ago and I inherited $500,000, and I really don't know what I should be doing with the money."

*You*:    **"What do you want the money to do for you?"**

*Jane*:  "Well, I really haven't put much away for retirement, so I guess I should probably be using it for that."

*You*:  **"When do you want to retire?"**

*Jane*:  "Yesterday. I really don't like my work that much. I would love not to have to work. So the sooner I could retire, the better."

*You*:  **"So if I could put together a program that would give you enough money to retire with your current lifestyle, how would that help you in the long run?"**

*Jane*:  "I could spend time doing what I really want to do and not spend so much of my time kissing people's 'you know whats' in order to make a living."

*You*:  **"What do you really want to spend your time doing** if you had total choice?"

*Jane*:  "I want to work with underprivileged children. It seems to me that there are so many children who don't get the love and encouragement they need to really make something of themselves. If I could really impact a handful of underprivileged children and help them be stronger members of society, that would make me feel pretty good."

*You*:  **"So if I could put together a program that would allow you to retire as soon as possible, so you could spend your time working with under-privileged children and really impact their lives, that would make you feel pretty good?"**

*Jane*:  "You got it!"

*You*:     "Well, let's see what we can do...."

Talking with Jane was relatively easy because she knew what she wanted and why it was important, and I didn't have to ask too many questions to get all the information. I used the Long Run Question to get her to visualize what she wanted in the future. Then she told me what was important and how she felt about it all at once, so I didn't have to ask her any more feeling-oriented questions. Instead, I put everything together in a Summary Question, including that it would "make her feel pretty good." I could have asked her more feeling questions and it would have still worked, but it felt like overkill in this case. I trusted my intuitive instincts.

The sequence of questions was:

1. **What's important**?
   "What do you want the money to do for you?"
2. **Qualifying Question**:
   "When do you want to retire?"
3. **Long Run Question:**
   "So if I could ... how would that help you in the long run?"
4. **Qualifying Question**:
   "What do you want to spend your time doing ...?"
5. **Summary Question:**
   "So if I could ... that would make you feel pretty good?"


## SPEND YOUR TIME WITH PEOPLE WHO CARE

It is important to see that when you are helping people determine what is most important to them and why, they can answer in any way they want to. You are not leading them to a conclusion, you are helping them get clear about what *they* want. For example, if it turns out that John doesn't feel obligated or responsible for taking care of his family, you don't have much of a client. You are not going to teach John to love his family in a one-hour fact-finding interview. The same would be true in the estate tax example. If Jerry really didn't care if the $1.2 million went to the government, there is not much point in going any further with him. Move on to the next person. Remember, you are after the truth about how people really feel. Sure, you can educate people on the options available and you may try for a different kind of sale, but you are not going to change someone's values in a couple meetings. You need to be able to recognize when you are "dead in the water" and move on to more qualified prospective clients.

In the examples I have given, everything worked out. The reality in the field is that some people care and some don't. The ones who care are the ones worth spending time with. Let the others go and you will be much happier and much wealthier.

## USING THE FEELING INFORMATION IN THE CLOSE

Have you ever noticed that you can do a great job getting people to a feeling level in the factfinder but have difficulty getting prospective clients back to the feeling level in a closing presentation that may be weeks later? You shouldn't have this problem anymore.

One of the first things you do in your closing presentation after some small talk is to review the main interests and motives of your prospective client. You might say: "Gene, I would like to take a minute to review what we talked about last time. You said the most important thing you wanted was to guarantee a college education for your two children. You said that you couldn't go to college and it took you a lot longer to establish yourself and get a good paying job. You feel you lost a lot of money as a result of not having a college education. You said that life is hard enough without having disadvantages, and that you want your children to have every possible advantage so they can have the security of good jobs. Do I have that right, Gene?"

Remember to use your prospective clients' exact words and to get this information written out so you can read it when you do your closing presentation. Also important toward the beginning of a closing presentation is to get a confirmation from your prospective clients that there is a problem to solve and that they want to solve it before you offer a solution or recommendations. If your prospective clients waiver in their commitment to what they said they wanted, you repeat what they said was important and why it was important, and ask them if anything has changed. If nothing has changed in terms of what they wanted, then something else is holding them back, which you can then attempt to isolate.

Knowing what your prospective clients want and why they want it gives you some powerful leverage in the closing presentation, but from a different perspective than you might expect. You can remind your prospective clients of what *they* said they wanted. It isn't what *you* said they *should* have. Most important is to remember that it is your job to help your prospective clients make the decision that feels intuitively right to them, which may include not doing anything.

Yes, you invite, intrigue, educate, show options, and weigh alternatives, but the final decision needs to feel right to your prospective clients. The real leverage that you have is your commitment to helping them make the decision that feels right to them after everything is said and done. You can be a lot more aggressive about the whole process if you are willing to walk away with nothing, if that is the decision that feels truly right to your prospective client. You did your job!

Actually, you will rarely walk away with nothing using this approach. The key difference is that you make the sale because your prospective clients *want* to buy for their reasons rather than wanting to "think about it" because they got maneuvered into a corner by your reasons. Focus on helping your prospective clients make the decision that feels right to them, and you can't lose. Yes, some people are going to choose not to buy at this time, but you will make more sales overall with this approach than with any other. Try it for 90 days. Your increased results and your increased self-esteem will make it hard to go back to the old ways.

**"LET ME THINK ABOUT IT"**

"Let me think about it" is not something that you are going to be thrilled to hear from your prospective clients, no matter what approach you use. But if you have done your job in helping your prospective clients determine what plan of action feels right to them, wanting to sleep on it may be a legitimate request. What I would want to know before I leave the meeting is this:

*You*:    "John, is there any reason not to go ahead with what we have come up with here?"

*John*:   "Well, I think I would like to give it a couple of days and get back to you."

*You*:    "Okay, John, that's fine. Let me ask you, **does the plan feel right to you?**"

*John*:    "Yes."

*You*:    "Do you see any reason not to go ahead with it in a couple of days?"

*John*:    "No. At this point I think we're on the right track."

*You*:    "**When should we plan on meeting?**"

The sequence of questions was:

1. **Does it feel right?**
   "Let me ask you: Does the plan feel right to you?"
2. **Any reason not to go ahead?**
   "Do you see any reason not to go ahead with it in a couple days?"
3. **Set up the next meeting:**
   "When should we plan on meeting?"

Maybe you could get John to take some other step toward completing the sale without making a full commitment at this point, like getting examined, or doing some paperwork. This is a matter of style and will differ with each salesperson. The most important thing is to get confirmation that what you have proposed feels right to them and they see no problems. Then be sure to set up the next step.

By now, you should be getting a sense of what it sounds like and feels like to get to a feeling level. Since people are all so different and so complex, you have to be ready for a variety of responses to your questions. Chapter Six is designed to help prepare you for some of the contingencies.

# *Chapter 6*

# TROUBLESHOOTING

## PREPARING YOURSELF
## TO ASK FEELING QUESTIONS

### Make a Commitment

First of all, you have to believe in the need to find out what is important to your prospective clients and why they feel that way. I am assuming that you agree that this information is required to do the job right, or you wouldn't have read this far. So what's left is to *make a commitment to getting to the feeling level with your prospective clients.* A commitment doesn't mean that you already know how you are going to do it, have everything figured out, and feel totally comfortable with the process. Quite the contrary. You may not know exactly how you are going to go about getting the feeling information. You are probably a long way from having it figured out, and you may not be very comfortable with the thought of asking the feeling questions. You don't need to have any of those things in order to be committed. Being committed simply says that you are going to achieve the goal one way or another, and you will learn what you need to know as you go along. There. That wasn't so hard, was it?

### Create a Target

Next, you have to prepare yourself from a creative standpoint. In order to create something new, whether it be tangible or, as in this case, a new behavior, you first have to *create a target vision or target feeling about what you want to create.* If you were to envision yourself being successful at asking the feeling-oriented questions, what would that be like? Imagine that you are creating a video in your mind of yourself and your prospective clients. What would you put in this video of you successfully and confidently asking your prospective clients the feeling-level questions? What do you see? What do you say to each other? What does it feel like when you are asking the questions? What does it feel like when you are waiting for them to answer? What does it feel like after you have had a successful interview? Make it real in your mind, make it positive, and it will happen.

**Trust Your Instincts and Take Action**

The next step is more subtle. You have to take action, but you also have to *trust your intuitive instincts as you take action*. (For detailed information on trusting your intuitive instincts, read my book *Trusting Yourself*.) If you are in the middle of an interview and it feels terribly wrong to ask someone a feeling-oriented question, you have some soul-searching to do. Are you avoiding asking the feeling-level questions because you are risking outside your comfort zone? In which case it may not feel totally *comfortable* asking the feeling-level questions, but it does *feel right* to ask them. If this is what you are feeling, you need to jump in and ask away. Otherwise, if it doesn't feel right to ask the feeling-level questions, you are either not in rapport or there is no chemistry, which means you are not in front of a qualified prospective client and it is probably time to wind up this interview and get on to the next one.

**Maintain a Neutral to Positive Attitude**

The last and crucial step of creating something new is to *maintain a neutral to positive attitude about whatever happens and learn from what happens*. There is no way to ask feeling-level questions perfectly. When you are dealing with people, you are dealing with an entity that is extremely complex and unpredictable. Asking feeling-oriented questions is an art, not a science. The only way to learn it is to dive in, start asking, and see what happens. It's like learning to ride a bicycle or learning how to swim. No matter how much you know intellectually, at some point you have to risk not knowing what you are going to do next and learn from experience. The most important thing at this point is to give yourself a lot of credit for risking something new and trust that whatever happens is exactly what needs to happen to get you to the next level.

## Role-Play First

Before you go charging off to ask some feeling-level questions, there are some other ways to increase the likelihood of success. *Role-play* with as many different friendly sources as you can first. Tell them what you are doing. Have them read some of the examples. When you start to feel that asking the feeling-level questions isn't that big of a deal, you are making progress.

## Pick Some "Trial Run" Candidates

After you have done some role-playing, *pick two or three trial run candidates* to interview. These are people who would fall into the C category of your client rating system. Get some practice on your Cs before you talk to your A and B clients or prospects. If you are newer to sales and you can't imagine a prospective client you don't care that much about, think in terms of having *no expectations*. Go interview three people and make an agreement with yourself that you are not going to be concerned about the results of what happens with these three people. They are simply for practice. It's okay if you happen to make a sale from your practice interviews. You just have to be careful that you are not hoping you will make a sale or the interviews won't be for practice anymore.

## Use a "Cheat Sheet"

*Make a "cheat sheet"* of the questions you want to ask. You can have more questions than you actually use. I always like to feel out the situation and pick the questions that seem the most right to me for that situation. If you have studied this material and role-played with some friends, you will know what kind of response you are after and will have a sense of what questions will give you that information. Your challenge at this point is to get to the appointment, establish rapport, relax, breathe, and ask the questions that feel right when the time feels right. I can hear someone saying, "How will I know when the time is right?" Again, relax, take a deep breath, and trust your instincts. Only one of two things can happen: You will either ask a question and it will work brilliantly or you will ask a question that doesn't work very well. The only way to find out what doesn't work is to experiment. As unorthodox as it sounds, having experiences that don't quite work are often better teachers than having only experiences that do work.

Which brings up another important point. If you ask a question and it bombs, don't be afraid to say, "That question didn't work. Let me ask you a different question." I have personally said that exact thing numerous times and I consider myself fairly skilled at this process. Remember, when you are interacting with people, *nothing works all the time*. The important thing to remember is if you are doing something that isn't working in a particular interview, refocus on what you want to learn from your prospective client and try another question.

## STILL NOT SURE WHAT QUESTIONS TO ASK?

Keep it simple. There are five key questions involved in getting to a feeling level presented in this material. The first two questions are **What's most important?** and **Why is that important to _YOU_?** (As I said earlier, if you just ask these two questions, you are way ahead of the crowd.) Then the second phase is to get your prospective clients to **describe in greater detail** what they say they want. Ask them if they can **get a sense** of what it would be like to have all that. And then, finally, would that be an **important feeling for them to have?**

The five key questions are:

1. **What's** (most) **important to you?**
2. **Why is that important to _YOU_?**
3. (Visualize the future) **Can you describe what it would be like** to have …?
4. **Can you get a sense** of what it would be to have …?
5. Would that be **an important feeling for you to have?**

These questions are not the only way to get to a feeling level in a sales interview. There are certainly many ways to accomplish the same purpose. Experiment. Trust your instincts. If a question doesn't feel right to you, don't ask it. What _will_ happen if you risk asking these questions is you will discover your own version of what works for you, and that's what we are really after.

Also realize that you will not have to ask every prospective client all of these questions. There are some people you will only have to ask, "What is important to you?" and they will give you the answers to all five questions so fast you will have to go back and make sure you got the information right. The main objective is to make sure you get to the feeling-level information with each prospective client one way or another.

## STILL UNCOMFORTABLE
## WITH THE QUESTIONS?

About two years into my life insurance career, I was assigned to a new sales manager by the name of Phil Kline. Phil had been a successful life insurance agent for a number of years and had also spent 15 years with the Dale Carnegie organization both teaching and selling their courses prior to getting into life insurance. I could tell right away that Phil was a gifted sales trainer, and I felt I could trust him to really help me.

Shortly after we first started to work together, I came back to the office one day full of excitement about a disability case I had just opened. The conversation went like this:

*Sid*:   "Boy, did I open a nice disability case with a doctor today!"

*Phil*:   "Great! Tell me about it."

*Sid*:   "Well, he was a referral, so I got right in to see him. We talked for a while about a variety of things, and it turned out that his disability coverage was what was most important to him at this point and it needed to be increased."

*Phil*:   "Why does he want disability coverage?"

*Sid*:   "He wants to protect his income in case he is sick or injured."

*Phil*:   "Good. And why does he want to protect his income in case he is sick or injured?"

*Sid*:   "Ah (long pause), I'm not sure."

*Phil*:    "Go back and find out."

At this point I was in a state of shock. I had succeeded in looking like I knew what I was doing with a referral to a doctor, and now Phil wanted me to go back and find out why he wanted to protect his income in case he was sick or injured. Isn't that enough of a reason all by itself? Not to Phil.

Going back to ask the doctor a question with such an obvious answer was not something I was looking forward to. But I did it and I was surprised at what happened. I eventually got around to asking the doctor why he wanted to protect his income and he said: "I see people who are sick and injured from all kinds of things every day. I know firsthand what the likelihood is of getting sick or injured. I don't want to risk my family's livelihood with those kinds of odds against me without as much protection as I can get." He bought a large policy to add to the coverage he already had.

Once I experienced what happened when I went to the feeling level with the doctor, it occurred to me that I had a number of other clients and cases that had not closed that I needed to get back to. By going back and getting to the feeling level with several cases I hadn't been able to close, I actually made a couple of sales with people I had given up on. I even went back to see a client who had bought only a month before, asked him the feeling-oriented questions, and he bought more! I was amazed and forever a believer. And the best news of all: My closing ratio doubled and stayed at that level from then on.

It's okay to be a little uncomfortable at first asking the feeling-level questions. The main thing to ask yourself is if it "feels right" for you to get to the feeling level with your prospective client. If your answer is yes, you won't be uncomfortable for very long. It only takes a couple of times to get the hang of it and get hooked. Plus, I will confidently predict that you will be well paid for asking a few more questions.

## WHAT IF THEY SAY "I DON'T KNOW"?

You are going to ask people feeling-level questions and some of them are going to respond by saying "I don't know." What "I don't know" or "I'm not sure" usually means is that your prospective clients are not clear about what they want on a conscious level. What they want is in their awareness somewhere. Your job is to help them get at it.

For example:

*You*:      "Ron, you have said that retirement planning is your most important concern at this point. You know retirement planning is important to a lot of people these days. Why is it important to *YOU*?"

*Ron*:      "Well, I'm not sure."

*You*:      "Have you thought about what you want to do at retirement?"

*Ron*:      "Well, not much, really."

*You*:      (With a laugh and a smile) "Well, Ron, do you think you are going to sit around, drink beer, and watch TV for most of your retirement?"

*Ron*:      (Now smiling) "Well, that doesn't sound too bad actually, but I think there are some other things I would want to be able to do."

*You:*    (Sincerely) "What do you want to be able to do, Ron?"

Something to remember about the way most of us have been trained to think: We know more about what we *don't* want than what we *do* want. But guess what you have to know in order to know what you don't want? What you do want. So I simply made something up that I knew would not be what Ron would want to do all the time during retirement. As it turned out, he said it didn't sound too bad. Finding out what people really want is always a great adventure!

## WHAT IF THEY WON'T ANSWER MY QUESTIONS?

First of all, if you are in rapport with your prospective clients, they will *want* to answer your questions because it is of great interest to them and they are starving for someone to really listen to what they have to say. Your prospective clients won't experience themselves as going through a sales interview in order to be sold something if you are doing your job right. They will feel like they are being asked legitimate questions that are required to determine the best possible plan of action by a trusted counselor-advisor. You are demonstrating that you care about what they have to say because you want to make sure that they get what they really want.

If you have taken the time to get into rapport and you feel some chemistry with your prospective clients, the likelihood of them not wanting to answer the feeling-level questions is extremely small. However, if this actually does happen, you probably don't have a qualified prospective client and should politely wind up the interview and move on. Something major is wrong if your prospective clients don't want to answer your questions. They may be hiding something. They may be embarrassed to tell you the truth. They may feel the details of the situation are too complex to get into. They may not want to share the details of the situation with anyone. They may feel that they can't share how they feel because of the "politics" involved with other people. Whatever the reason, it's risky to work with someone who can't tell you what's important and why. Not that it can't be done. It is actually done more often than we might think. The problem is that the business could go out the door as fast as it came in for reasons you will never know. You have to decide if you are comfortable with that level of risk. Especially if you get paid an annualized commission.

So what can you do if you are in the middle of an interview and all of a sudden your prospective clients won't answer your feeling-level questions? One approach is to *tell them how you would answer the questions for yourself.* This allows you to share your feelings about how you feel toward a similar situation. This gives your prospective clients an idea of the kind of answer you are looking for. It also gets you expressing your feelings *first* which is all some people need to feel safe. If this doesn't work, you may have to get tougher. Tell the truth about the situation gently but firmly: "John and Mary, I'm afraid I can't be of any help to you if you won't answer my questions. I am sorry if I've made you uncomfortable in any way, but I am just trying to do the best job possible for you. Are you uncomfortable with the questions I am asking you? Maybe I could rephrase the question. Maybe this isn't the best time for us to be talking. Maybe I'm just not the right person to be talking to you about these matters." Hopefully at this point they will shift and open up. If they don't, you have to decide if it feels right to continue the process without the feeling-level information.

If you really care about helping your prospective clients make the decision that feels right to them, you will take the time to create a safe environment for them to talk in. Under these conditions, it would be rare for someone you want as a client not to answer your questions.

## I DON'T WANT TO BE MANIPULATIVE

I did a sales training for a company that wholesaled car batteries in the late 1970s. They had about 10 salespeople, most of whom were experienced. I developed a question-oriented sales track for them to use with their prospective clients. We were meeting once a week for several weeks. The third week into the program, one of the salespeople was sharing his experience with the sales track since the last meeting. He said, "You know this question-oriented sales track isn't really fair. I didn't have anyone say no to me all week long!"

It's amazing to me that some people believe that if we somehow know what questions to ask, we can get people to do something they don't want to do. Even if this were possible, why would you want to do it? What really *does* work the majority of the time is to ask people a series of questions that help them define what they really want. And if you can show them that you can honestly provide what they want, why would they say no? It isn't manipulative to find out what people want and then help them get it. People want to buy! *We are so brainwashed by our sales culture into thinking that we have to lead, corner, trick, cajole, or otherwise outsmart our prospective clients, or they won't buy anything. Nothing is further from the truth.*

Your job is to identify interested prospective clients, find out what they are trying to accomplish, educate them on what the options are, and then get them to make a decision on what feels right to them. That is not manipulation. That is brilliant problem solving. If you are using the approach I just described and very few people are saying no to you, it isn't because you are forcing them into a corner. It is because you are helping them get what they really want and they are responding by buying!

Remember, we've been brought up in a sales culture that says it's more important to make the sale than to help our prospective clients make the decision that feels right to them. Some would argue that you are trying to *both* make a sale *and* help prospective clients get what they want. The problem is that once the goal of making the sale becomes more important than the well-being of the client, we are slipping into the fear-based Robber Baron paradigm, which will spell trouble in the long run.

If all of a sudden you start to have a lot of people saying yes because you are helping them get clear about what they want and then helping them get it, you should be celebrating! Having people say yes because they are getting what they really want is not manipulation. It's the breakthrough to a paradigm of trust and abundance.

## CONQUERING THE CHALLENGE OF CHANGE

Why is it so difficult to change the way we naturally tend to do things?

### The Subconscious Survival Mind

There is a powerful part of our brain that is in charge of our survival. In my other publications, I have referred to this part of our awareness as the "survival mind." Some experts say that the survival function is part of the subconscious mind. For this discussion, let's combine the two names and call it the "subconscious survival mind."

Where does the subconscious survival mind get its information on what is safe and what is a threat to our survival?

Some information we simply inherit as basic human needs such as breathing, eating, eliminating, sleeping, etc. Some information we are taught by parents and other authority figures as children. Finally, a large portion of the information we have about what is best for our survival is learned from our experiences in life.

The subconscious survival mind learns from our experiences in life through one basic approach. It likes to monitor our behavior (activity) and determine if what we have done worked or didn't work in relation to our survival. If we have acted in a way that the subconscious survival mind determines is a threat to our survival, we are going to experience a lot of resistance if we try to repeat that behavior. Try seeing how long you can hold your breath before your mind starts to question what you are doing and how long you plan on doing it.

On the other hand, if we act in a particular way and the subconscious survival mind sees that our survival was *not* threatened, that behavior becomes an accepted approach. Notice that it doesn't matter to the subconscious survival mind if the behavior produced the result we are after. The key to the subconscious survival mind is simply whether our survival was threatened or not. If we survived, that particular behavior is okay to use again. This approach creates a fascinating phenomenon that only humans (as opposed to other animals) seem to do: *We will more readily repeat behaviors that we have experienced as not being a threat to our survival before we will risk an unfamiliar behavior that would clearly work better.*

## Of Mice and Men

A way to observe this phenomenon would be to create a series of six parallel dead-end tunnels several feet long which emanate from a common starting area. Put a piece of cheese at the end of the last tunnel or the one farthest away. Put a mouse in the common area where there is access to all the tunnels, but put it in front of the tunnel that is the farthest away from the tunnel with the cheese. Assuming that the mouse can't smell the cheese at the starting point, it will proceed to check out each tunnel *only once* until it finds the cheese. Humans (with their unique capacity to reason) put in the similar situation will often demonstrate the peculiar tendency of continuing to go down the same tunnel with no cheese simply because they have determined a particular tunnel (behavior) to be safe and familiar. With the belief that "the cheese must be there somewhere and I just don't see it," some humans would never get out of the first tunnel with no cheese. Our ability to reason is incredibly powerful, but it can obviously also get in our way if we lose touch with the bigger picture.

## Perceived Threats Feel Real

Another important characteristic of how the subconscious survival mind works is that a *perceived  threat* is as dangerous as an actual threat. Which basically means we can experience resistance to certain behaviors where there is no real threat, simply a perceived one. (The word *FEAR* used as an acronym stands for False Evidence Appearing Real.) As a peak performance coach to hundreds of life insurance agents, I have helped a lot of agents conquer their call reluctance. With call reluctance, there is no real threat to our survival, but the actual experience of dialing the telephone for someone with severe call reluctance is very similar to what you would feel if you were swimming in the ocean and all of a sudden you saw a shark fin heading directly for you at a high rate of speed. You would want to be somewhere else really fast. Perceived threats and real threats create similar feelings of fear.

What gets formed out of all this monitoring of behavior by our subconscious survival mind is what is often referred to as a "comfort zone." Any behavior within the comfort zone is acceptable to the subconscious survival mind. Anything proven to be a threat or a perceived threat is to be avoided. And since the subconscious survival mind is very powerful, it can be rather difficult to experiment with any behaviors outside of our comfort zone.

## CREATING SOME ROOM TO EXPERIMENT

So if asking feeling-oriented questions is outside of your current comfort zone, what can you do to give yourself some room to experiment?

### Role-Play

First of all, it helps if you can ease yourself into it. As I have previously mentioned, *role-play*. Practice with family and friends. Then you can set up some interviews where you decide beforehand that you don't care what happens. This will give your subconscious mind some positive experience with asking the feeling-oriented questions so that you will start to question whether asking feeling-oriented questions is really as bad as you thought it was.

## The Swiss Cheese Method

Another approach is the *Swiss Cheese Method*. Here, you at least put a dent in what you are trying to accomplish by doing *something* in the direction you want to go. In your next interview, at least find out *what* is most important to your prospective client and *why* that would be important. If you have a positive experience, that will make a major contribution to your ability to ask even more feeling-oriented questions next time. If you have a less than positive experience, you have to trust that the rapport or chemistry wasn't there and try again with your next appointment. If you are with the right people and they are open enough toward you to give you a chance, they are going to answer whatever questions you ask them. Sometimes your prospective clients may "test the water" a little by initially giving you a vague answer to your feeling-oriented questions. In this case you can simply ask for greater detail so that you are sure you understand what they mean.

If asking feeling-oriented questions is outside your comfort zone, you have to ease your subconscious survival mind into seeing that there is no danger by creating some positive experiences. Also, it is equally of value to have your subconscious survival mind see that even an attempt to get to a feeling level that doesn't go as smoothly as you would like isn't anything to be overly concerned about. But you still have to ask some feeling-oriented questions in order to find that out.

## The Power to Choose

One other thing that has been of great help to me in changing behaviors is to realize that *we create our experience of what happens to us.* We actually have to choose to have the emotional feelings about what happens to us. This was a major revelation to me when I finally saw this for myself. I always thought that my emotional feelings were something that just happened and that I didn't have any control over them. For example, if someone did something that made me angry, it seemed normal and logical to respond to them by being angry. I was amazed to discover that I actually have to *choose* to be angry in order to be angry. And the reason I know this is because I can also choose not to be angry in a split second if I want to and choose to experience something else. I can choose not to care. I can choose to ignore the situation. I can choose to be upset because people are not always the way I would like them to be. I can choose to laugh or make a joke about the situation. I can choose to analyze why I want to feel angry, and so on. I have a lot more options in a given moment than I ever realized.

The problem with anger and other emotions is that they happen so fast, we don't have the experience that we have chosen to feel the way we do. It appears to just happen out of our control. So if you ask a feeling-oriented question and you start to feel stupid for asking it, remember that you are choosing to feel stupid. You can choose another feeling. You can choose not to have any emotional feelings about what is happening. Just ask the questions and see what happens. You will learn *what works and what doesn't* in the shortest amount of time if you give yourself some room to experiment. Forget about doing it perfectly and choose not to feel one way or another emotionally. *Stay neutral.* Remember, when you are dealing with people, nothing works all the time. You can do things "perfectly" and people can and will give you the "wrong" response. You have to be ready to try something else if what you are doing isn't working and not think another thought about it.

# Chapter 7

## HELPFUL
## HINTS
## FROM
## A
## BIGGER
## PERSPECTIVE

## BETTER LIVING THROUGH CHEMISTRY

There is more business out there for you than you could ever write if you worked 24 hours a day for *three* lifetimes. You might as well be selective and work with people you enjoy working with. This factor can be the difference between loving your work and putting up with your work. Give yourself the gift of only working with people where the chemistry is obviously there. Give all the other leads to your colleagues.

Said a little differently, you have a choice. You can make your job about finding those people who are ready for you and want to do something. Or you can pursue whoever will talk to you and see if you can get them to buy something. You can make a good living with either choice, except the first choice is a lot of fun and the second is a lot of work.

## DON'T ASSUME YOUR PROSPECTIVE CLIENTS KNOW WHAT THEY WANT

Don't fall into the trap of assuming that your prospective clients have thought long and hard about what they want and why they want it. They do know what they want and why, but it may not be very conscious or clear. Besides, many of your prospective clients will tend to put off thinking about insurance- and investment-related discussions until they are asked to do so. That is why it is so important to take people through the feeling-oriented questions. *They* need to hear what they have to say as much as *you* need to hear it.

One of the biggest mistakes I see financial services salespeople make on a regular basis is that once they start to learn the motivations for why people buy certain financial products, they tend to assume that their prospective clients know what they want and why they want it. After all, if you're a prospective client, you must know what you want and why you want it, right? The reality is that most people have *some* idea about what they want, but they need to have a conversation with someone who can ask them the right questions and show them the appropriate options in order to crystallize their thinking and create a course of action that feels right. Then they can make a commitment. Don't assume. Ask questions!

## WHAT IF I RUN OUT OF PROSPECTS?

There is never a shortage of qualified people to see, only the illusion that there is a shortage. To prove this to yourself, call all your current prospects, even the ones you've been saving until the time is just right. Call 'em all. Get them to make a decision one way or another. You will discover that there are always more qualified prospects even though your fears may tell you otherwise. Sometimes you have to make room for new prospects by getting rid of the old ones who can't seem to make a decision one way or the other. Trust that the new qualified prospects will show up even if you have no idea where they will come from at this moment. Some call this a gutsy approach. Some call it a matter of trust.

## THE IDEAL RELATIONSHIP
## BETWEEN YOU AND YOUR CLIENT

Have your focus be to help your clients make the decision that feels right to them combined with the knowledge of your expertise and experience. Remember that when making the sale becomes more important than helping your prospective clients make the decision that feels right to them, you are operating in a negative, fear-based context,

which by definition has to produce negative results somewhere.

A high closing ratio that you can be proud of should come
from your skill as a counselor and helping people get what
they really want, rather than from your ability to back
people into a corner and overpower or outsmart them into a
sale.

## BE YOURSELF

To attract the clients you really want to work with, be who
you most enjoy being when you are with anyone who could
become a client. Experience yourself as a human being
instead of a job title or job description. When you make a
prospecting call or go to an interview, be the same person
you would be if you were going to have lunch with
someone you cared for a great deal. You *are* the same
person!

## THE MORE YOU CARE

The more you care about helping people get what they
really want, the more you will be compelled to ask the
feeling-oriented questions. You will lose your fear of
asking the questions. You will lose your fear of not knowing how people will respond or of what they will say.
Helping people clarify what they want that feels right will
become such an overriding mission that any apprehension
or hesitation toward asking feeling-level questions will first
become unimportant and then disappear altogether.

Do you remember the first time you asked someone how
much money he or she made? In most cases, if you're in the
financial services business, you have to know how much

money people make and what they are doing with it. Even though there is a very logical explanation for asking the question, that doesn't make it any easier the first few times if you have never asked the question before. But after a few times it gets a lot easier. Fairly soon, asking the highly personal question of how much money someone made last year becomes a routine part of doing a good job. Asking feeling-oriented questions follows the same sequence to eventually become a routine part of doing a good job. The most important thing is to get the first few times you ask feeling-oriented questions out of the way.

## YOU CAN LEAD A HORSE TO WATER ...

The old saying "You can lead a horse to water, but you can't make him drink" has an application in selling. If you want the sale more than your prospective client does, you're going to have to put a lot of extra energy into making the sale. The real problem is that after the sale is made, you will continue to have to put that same extra energy into keeping that business on the books. In the long run it isn't worth the effort to have to keep reselling someone something they didn't want in the first place. Find a more qualified prospective client.

## YOU LEARN MORE FROM YOUR MISTAKES

Be willing to make mistakes. It is the quickest way to learn what works and what doesn't work. If your intention is positive and you are conscientious in your desire to do the right thing, the negative effect of your mistakes will be minimal. In some cases, you will find that your mistakes are your most brilliant moves.

When you are interacting with people, nothing works all the time. If something you are doing isn't working that worked with someone else, try something else.

If you ask a question and it bombs, simply say that was the wrong question and try another. If you are in rapport with your prospective clients, *they want the interview to go well as much as you do.*

## THE CHALLENGE OF PARADOX

If you really want to be good at selling and enjoy every aspect of a selling career at the same time, you have to embrace a challenging paradox. On the one hand, you have to be willing to give 100% of everything you know to do to get people to make the decision that feels right to them. On the other hand, you can't care who buys and who doesn't. Remember, I said to be good and enjoy *every* aspect of selling, which must include some people not buying. Believe it or not, you can actually be empowered by a prospective client not buying anything if that is the decision that really feels right to him or her.

I can hear someone saying: "What do you mean you don't care who buys and who doesn't buy! How can you not care? This is your livelihood we are talking about here!" I understand. Remember, though, it is a paradox. Do everything you know how to do to get your prospective clients to make the decision that feels right to them and then trust who buys and who doesn't. I realize this approach may take some getting used to. But it is also the approach that will bring you the greatest happiness and self-fulfillment (which has to include an abundant income, since being poor is not self-fulfilling for most people).

## THE POWER OF INTUITION

Trust your intuitive instincts. You will find them an awesome direction finder, but you have to remember to ask yourself questions and trust that the answers will come.

If you aren't sure if you have intuitive instincts, relax all the tension out of your body and your mind. (If you have trouble with this, imagine for a moment that nothing matters, no one cares, and money is not an issue.) Be willing to believe that there is always an answer to whatever question you might have. Take a deep breath or two. Now ask yourself: "If I had intuitive instincts, what would they feel like? How would I recognize them? When have things just felt right to me in the past?" Simply ask yourself the questions you want answers to in a relaxed state of trust and you will get the answers you seek. Don't be discouraged if you don't sense an answer right away. Trust that the answer is on the way and that it will arrive in time. (Read the section on intuition in my book *Trusting Yourself*.)

One of my most fascinating discoveries as a peak performance coach is that quantum leaps in production rarely come from intellectually "figuring out" what to do. They come from trusting and acting on your intuitive instincts, which will show you things that you would never have "figured out." That's why they are quantum leaps. They are beyond the perspective of our currently available intellectual knowledge. However, once you discover something that creates a quantum leap for you, you won't understand how you could have missed something so obvious.

## BE SOLUTION-ORIENTED

In our society it is normal and accepted to have a negative perspective on things. It is normal to think and talk in terms of "what's wrong" and "why we need to fix it." I noted earlier that most people know more about what they *don't* want than what they *do* want. Negativity is normal and accepted because it is very predictable. It is much easier to put our faith in Murphy's Law, which states, "If anything can go wrong it will." The unfortunate consequence of our tendency toward negative "what's wrong" thinking is that we become problem-oriented rather than solution-oriented. We tend to look at a problem and then become defensive with a goal of trying to minimize the potential damage. Being solution-oriented, on the other hand, is quite different. Rather than getting bogged down in the negative things that could happen, you simply say to yourself, "What would be a workable solution to this situation?"

I was listening in on a conversation a colleague of mine was having with a client of his recently on this subject. He said to his client: "You are asking yourself the wrong question. Don't ask yourself what you are going to do if you don't make enough money. Ask yourself how you can make sure you will make more money than you need."

## TRUST THE PROCESS

Trust the creative process of life. If you have a vision or feeling about what you want to create and you let life teach you how to reach your goal by your experiences, it is only a matter of time before your vision becomes a reality. Of course, some visions take longer than others. Be careful not to get so obsessed with reaching your goal that you miss the little lessons that life is trying to teach you. The critical breakthroughs are often tiny little things that you don't see until you relax and let go of trying to control every detail.

Once we start to take action toward making our vision a reality, all kinds of things happen. Some circumstances and events will appear to contribute to our success, some will appear to have no effect, and some will appear to be setbacks. Whatever happens, the key to "staying on a roll" and reaching your goal as quickly as possible is not to negatively judge what happens. Develop the capacity to observe what is happening from a neutral perspective. Look for the value and the "lessons" being presented by what is happening rather than judging whether it is good or bad, positive or negative. With a "neutral" perspective, we will more quickly see the information that is required for our ultimate success.

# Chapter 8

## WHAT'S
## IN
## IT
## FOR
## YOU?

## THE BENEFITS OF ASKING
## FEELING-ORIENTED QUESTIONS

Asking the feeling-oriented questions has many potential benefits. You could *double your income.* Many people have more than doubled their incomes by using the information presented in this book. There is also a large group of people who would prefer *more free time* to more income. I have had many clients double their free time and *still* have a substantial increase in income. If you have the positive intention of really wanting to help people achieve their financial goals and are willing to experiment and discover what new approaches really feel right to you, *good things are going to happen.* For every action taken with a positive intent, *momentum is building in your favor.* It is only a matter of time before *you will be compensated for your efforts.* However, you have to have some faith and trust in life's creative process while you patiently wait for the results to manifest.

*You will be rewarded for the courage* to take your prospective clients to a feeling level. You will find out that people really do want to answer feeling-oriented questions. You will discover that people are starving to share what they feel with someone who they sense cares about them as people and who is genuinely interested in what they have to say. You will find that people want to communicate at a deeper level with their advisors.

Once you experience the ability to intentionally get to the feeling level with your prospective clients and once you experience a much deeper level of relationship, *you will be hooked.* You will become aware when you don't have that deeper level of relationship with your prospective clients. You will miss the feeling of *being appreciated* for your courage and skill in asking feeling-oriented questions. You will notice when you have not gotten your prospective clients to the feeling level because they will have *much less of a sense of urgency* about taking action on your recommendations.

## GOOD THINGS HAPPEN

When you are over on "the same side of the table" as your prospective clients and help them determine what they really want, educate them on the best options, and help them make decisions that feel right to them, a lot of good things will happen.

- Your clients are going to appreciate, admire, and trust you more.

- The struggle begins to melt away. Your work becomes more empowering and fun to do.

- Good fortune will find you with increased frequency.

- You will feel increased self-esteem, a greater sense of professionalism, and a greater respect for the impact you have on the people you interact with. Your self-confidence will become unshakable in a peaceful way.

- You will be inspired by the energy generated from your relationships. As a friend of mine so profoundly put it, "If you're doing it right, you should end the day with more energy than when you started."

- You will find yourself being less serious and smiling and laughing more often.

- You will still have to prospect, but you will find that a deeper belief in the value of the work you do for people will help you maintain the edge that will keep you prospecting.

- There will still be setbacks and disappointments in life, but you will have more energy to deal with them and they won't seem as bad.

- The smiling faces and the words or gratitude that come from helping other people make choices that feel right to them will be an ongoing reminder of the power of this approach. Trust and act on what feels deeply right to you and you can cast aside the overcontrolled, uninspired routine that slowly burns us out for an empowering adventure that will keep you young at heart forever.

# *Appendices*

## REINFORCE YOUR COMMITMENT
## WITH A STUDY GROUP

Study groups have been proven to be a substantial contributing factor toward the growth and development of salespeople. The primary reason they can be so powerful is the same as that discussed in the rapport-building section on page 51 of this book. Shared experiences, and in particular shared feeling-level experiences, are the most powerful rapport builders between people. When feelings are shared, millions of pieces of information can be communicated in seconds. Everyone hears something of value when someone shares his or her experience on a feeling level.

There are several other keys to having successful study group meetings, including: having a designated group leader, ground rules or agreements on how to run the meetings, and a purpose for the meeting with an agenda of what is to be discussed.

You can choose a group leader for your next meeting at the end of each meeting. The group leader's job is to open and close the meeting, make logistical arrangements for the next meeting, and generally see to it that the purpose, agenda, and ground rules are followed to ensure the success of the meeting.

Having ground rules is more important with larger groups. The smaller the group, the more leniency there tends to be and therefore the need for ground rules diminishes. However, no matter what the size of your group, there are a few ground rules that I would recommend to ensure the success of your meeting. The following are some sample ground rules to get you started. You will want to make additions and/or deletions according to what your group decides is appropriate.

- Create a safe environment for all to share freely by not being critical of anyone or anything that is said in the meetings.

- Keep an open, neutral mind. Try not to judge anything that is said as right or wrong, good or bad; just let whatever is said be information that you may or may not use.

- Participate fully in whatever way you feel is most appropriate for you.

- If you are called on by the group leader or it is your turn to participate, and you do *not* want to participate, simply say, "I pass."

- (Optional, more important with larger groups) If you want to make a comment or ask a question of another group member, be recognized by the group leader.

- Be willing to get value from the meeting no matter what is said or discussed.

- Keep everything that is said confidential.

- Begin and end the meetings on time.

Having a stated purpose for your study group meetings is important because it gives the group a positive focus for the meeting, which substantially increases the likelihood of having a successful meeting. If the group members are aligned on the purpose of the meeting, you will have a good meeting. It's that simple. The purpose of your study group meeting can be general or specific. An example of a general purpose statement:

> *The purpose of our study group meetings is to enhance our skill level as professional salespeople, to share ways to increase our sales results with integrity, and to experience greater self-fulfillment from our work.*

Any number of topics can be discussed with the general purpose statement. You can pick different topics for each meeting, but make sure you include *getting prospective clients to a feeling level* as a part of each meeting or at least a frequent meeting topic. If you're meeting once a week, you can have a meeting about asking the feeling-level questions once a month. If you are meeting once a quarter or less, you will want to have getting to the feeling level be a regular part of your meetings.

An example of a specific purpose for a meeting that addresses *getting prospective clients to a feeling level*:

> *The purpose of this meeting is to increase our skill level in asking the feeling-level questions in a sales interview, to increase our comfort level in asking the feeling-level questions, and to increase the self-fulfillment we experience from our work as the result of asking the feeling questions.*

It is a good idea to have the group leader read the purpose for the meeting in addition to having the purpose written somewhere in front of the room or at the top of the meeting agenda to get everyone aligned on what the meeting is about.

From here you decide what your agenda is going to be. It is good to start meetings out with a "warmup" of some kind. A "warmup" is an exercise that gets everyone moving, talking, and interacting with each other. A fun warmup is to have everyone stand up, walk around, and take 20 seconds (10 seconds each way) to introduce themselves and say a sentence or two about themselves to each member of the group. You can have the group leader say "next" every 20 seconds until everyone has said hello to everyone else in the room. (The group leader should also say hello to everyone in addition to keeping track of the time for this exercise.)

If everyone knows each other, you can have each of the members start by standing up, introducing themselves, and then have them do either a brief announcement or quick summary of an article, book, tape program, seminar, etc., they feel would be of interest to the group.

The rest of the meeting should be primarily having the group members share their experiences and what they learned from them. You might ask participants to share what was the most rewarding experience they had getting prospective clients to a feeling level (since the last time you met) and what they learned from it. You may also want to set a time limit for how long people can share their experience. Whatever amount of time you choose to give people, have the group leader circle his or her finger in the air with the "wind it up" signal a few minutes before the end of the time limit. This gives everyone equal time to talk and a graceful way for participants to finish.

You will want to allow a little time after each person shares his or her experience for feedback or comments from the group. *Positive comments only.* Remember, there is really no such thing as "constructive criticism." Criticism in any form directed at what a study group member shares with the group will be destructive. Criticism is based on the premise that there is a right and a wrong way to do things and that the person doing the criticizing knows what is right and wrong. If you want to assure that you will walk away from your study group meetings empowered rather than "beaten up," don't allow "constructive criticism."

If you have time, you could go around and have everyone share his or her experience again on another subject, have selected people share an idea related to asking feeling questions, or share a sales idea. Follow the basic concepts presented here and you will have empowering meetings that are well worth the time you invest to attend them.

Study groups can be a powerful resource for helping you maintain the edge of peak performance. They are particularly useful for reminding us to ask the feeling questions, which we can easily stop asking if we are not reminded of their importance on a regular basis.

# *About the Author*

*Sidney C. Walker*

Sid Walker has proven to have an exceptional aptitude for coaching salespeople to quantum leaps in both their production and the self-fulfillment they get from their work. His expertise has evolved from over 14 years of "hands-on" experience as a peak performance coach working predominantly with top sales executives in the financial services field.

Sid is known for his extraordinary ability to identify the little things that make the difference between doing "okay" and "thriving." His specialty is helping salespeople customize their businesses to take maximum advantage of their natural style and strengths. The resulting increases in sales and self-esteem are outstanding.

Prior to embarking on his coaching career, Sid was a life insurance agent with Northwestern Mutual for four years, specializing in Disability Income Insurance. He has a multidisciplinary Bachelor of Arts degree from Michigan State University emphasizing Management and Psychology. Sid lives in Longmont, Colorado, with his wife, Linda, and their daughter, Madeline.

# *Other Products by Sid Walker*

## *TRUSTING YOURSELF*
### *How to Overcome the Psychological Barriers to Reaching Your Potential SELLING LIFE INSURANCE, INVESTMENTS AND FINANCIAL PLANNING SERVICES.*
(Book, 157 pp.)

## *THE PROSPECTING MENTALITY*
### *How to Get in the Right Frame of Mind to Prospect for New Business*
(**"THE CURE FOR CALL RELUCTANCE"** on Four Audio Cassettes)

# *For More Information*

For information on:

- **"in house" workshops**
- **individual coaching** (in person or by telephone)
- **ordering** books and tapes
- *quantity discounts* on books and tapes

### CALL:

High Plains Publications
Longmont, Colorado
800-323-6567
(24-hour answering service)